"This cookbook is deliciously stuffed with tradition and love."

> —Nia Vardalos,
> writer and star of
> *My Big Fat Greek Wedding*

"Greek food is so much more than just Spanakopita! Debbie proves that again and again with the recipes and photos in this book. She even shares her family secrets for perfect Greek meals and in turn gets in touch with her family history and heritage. This book is a must for anyone interested in experiencing the richness of the food and culture of Greece!"

> —Olympia Dukakis,
> Academy Award and
> Golden Globe winner

"Debbie has really captured the essence of the true Greek classics that are my soul food. The authentic recipes and delicious photos share the spirit of Greece on every page. It is a must-have for any cook."

> —Cat Cora, *Iron Chef*

"Like Debbie, my grandmother (Yiayia) always had something delicious and healthy waiting for us in the kitchen. I congratulate Debbie for gathering all these wonderful recipes together and never taking the gifts of tradition and good health for granted."

> —Melina Kanakaredes,
> star of *CSI: NY*

"I don't know anyone who embodies more fire, energy, and passion into their everyday life the way Debbie does. You can feel it on every page of this beautifully written and photographed cookbook. The recipes are easy to follow, and the food is absolutely amazing! It made my Greek husband homesick!"

> —Cristina Ferrare,
> *New York Times* bestselling
> author and cohost of Hallmark's
> Emmy-nominated *Home & Family*

IT'S ALL GREEK TO ME

TRANSFORM YOUR HEALTH THE MEDITERRANEAN WAY
WITH MY FAMILY'S CENTURY-OLD RECIPES

DEBBIE MATENOPOULOS

WITH **PETER CAPOZZI**

PHOTOGRAPHS BY JON FALCONE
FOREWORD BY MICHAEL OZNER, MD

BENBELLA BOOKS, INC.
DALLAS, TX

BenBella Books, Inc.
10300 N. Central Expressway
Suite #530
Dallas, TX 75231
www.benbellabooks.com
Send feedback to feedback@benbellabooks.com

Printed in the United States of America
10 9 8 7 6 5 4 3 2 1

Library of Congress Cataloging-in-Publication Data:

Matenopoulos, Debbie, author.
    It's all Greek to me : transform your health the
Mediterranean way with my family's century-old recipes /
by Debbie Matenopoulos with Peter Capozzi ; foreword by
Michael Ozner, MD.
        pages   cm
    Includes bibliographical references and index.
    ISBN 978-1-939529-93-0 (hardback)
    ISBN 978-1-939529-94-7 (electronic)
    1. Cooking, Mediterranean.   2. Cooking—Greece.
I. Title.
    TX725.M35M38   2014
    641.59'1822—dc23   2013043689

Editing by Trish Sebben-Krupka
Copyediting by Debra Manette
Proofreading by James Fraleigh and Kristin Vorce
Index by Clive Pyne Book Indexing Services
Additional photography by Meghan Capozzi Rowe
Cover design by Bradford Foltz
Jacket design by Sarah Dombrowsky
Printed by Bang Printing

Distributed by Perseus Distribution
www.perseusdistribution.com

To place orders through Perseus Distribution:
Tel: (800) 343-4499
Fax: (800) 351-5073
E-mail: orderentry@perseusbooks.com

Significant discounts for bulk sales are available.
Please contact Glenn Yeffeth at
glenn@benbellabooks.com or (214) 750-3628.

For my father,

NIKOLAOS "NIKO" MATENOPOULOS

You have always been my strength,
my courage, my laughter, my heart.

We all miss you very much, Baba.
Until we meet again . . .

December 6, 1940–March 7, 2012

A percentage of the proceeds from the sale
of this book will be donated directly to
the ALS Association with the hope
of finding a cure.

Contents

Foreword

Heart disease is the leading cause of death of men and women in America and worldwide. As a board-certified cardiologist, I have dedicated my life's work to the prevention of cardiovascular disease and its clinical manifestations of heart attack and stroke. I have seen firsthand how the highly processed, calorie-dense, and nutrient-depleted toxic American diet, along with a sedentary and stressful lifestyle, has amplified this disease in our country.

Unfortunately, our current approach to health care in America is failing. We're treating illness when it strikes but not preventing illness before it begins. The good news is there is a solution for preventing heart disease and lowering the risk of cancer and a long list of chronic degenerative diseases. In fact, you're already a step ahead of the game because you're reading this book! We simply need to look to the beautiful Mediterranean region for inspiration.

In my book *The Complete Mediterranean Diet,* I reference numerous medical studies that show how a Mediterranean diet, rich in delicious non-processed food from the land and the sea, is our best defense against chronic disease. In fact, this dietary pattern might just be our "fountain of youth." A recent study demonstrated that chromosome telomere shortening leads to aging, and a Mediterranean diet helps to slow this process. Another study from Boston, the Nurses' Health Study, found that greater adherence to a Mediterranean diet in midlife was related to nearly a 50 percent greater likelihood of surviving to seventy years or older with no major impairment in physical or mental health. Perhaps the most impressive trial was a landmark study from Spain that was recently reported in the prestigious *New England Journal of Medicine* (February 2013) comparing a Mediterranean diet to a low-fat diet. The study was stopped after 4.8 years due to a highly significant 30 percent reduction in major cardiovascular events (heart attack, stroke, death) in those following the Mediterranean diet. As reported in the *New York Times* on March 2, 2013, "This is a watershed moment in the field of nutrition . . . for the first time, researchers have shown that a diet can have an effect as powerful as drugs in preventing what really matters to patients—heart attacks, strokes, and death from cardiovascular disease."

While the medical studies are important, a Mediterranean diet and lifestyle is much more than simply clinical trials—it's a way of life that has existed for thousands of years. I am reminded of a man named Dimitrios, who lived his entire life on the Greek island of Crete. When asked to share his secret of longevity upon reaching one hundred years of age, he replied, "I walk every day, work in my garden, eat fresh food from the earth and sea, and I enjoy my midday meal with a glass of wine surrounded by my family and friends." Well, Dimitrios, I couldn't have said it any better.

In *It's All Greek to Me,* the charming Debbie Matenopolous puts these nutrition principles into practice, sharing rich, flavorful, heart-healthy recipes that have been passed down in her family from generation to generation. From *Spanakopita* to *Tzatziki, Fava* to *Baklava,* you'll find delicious, authentic dishes that have sustained the heart health of an entire region for centuries. In addition to opening her family's recipe book, Debbie also introduces readers to Greek culture through stories and photos, encouraging us to also adopt their vibrant way of life.

We have much to learn from Greek culture if we want to produce real change when it comes to America's health. Debbie has graciously opened her kitchen, inviting us into her Greek family and equipping us with menus to dramatically improve our health.

—Michael Ozner, MD, FACC, FAHA
    Medical Director,
    Center for Prevention and Wellness
    Baptist Health South Florida

Spice market, Athens.

Philotimo and the Greek Art of Living, Loving, Laughing, and . . . Eating Well

This book started with a simple idea. My mother is an amazing cook, so I wanted to write a cookbook with her and include all of our family recipes. For years people have asked me how I learned to cook so well. Many of my friends assumed I had gone to cooking school. That concept seems so strange to me. Of course I know how to cook. I'm Greek. Cooking is in our blood. Growing up in a traditional Greek home, I learned the art of Greek cooking simply by watching my yiayia, my mom, my aunts, my cousins, and my sister. That is precisely how my mother learned to cook, my mother's mother before her, and down the line for generations. That is how most Greeks learn to cook. It is a family affair. To Greeks, food is not just *food*. It represents love. It represents family. Sitting down to the table to eat is the time when friends and family come together to connect and share their day with one another, the good, the bad, and the ugly. The most impactful and poignant conversations of my childhood and young adult life all happened at the dinner table. This ritual is one of the most important ways that we Greeks keep such close-knit family bonds.

Because of this, spending time in the kitchen has never been stressful for me. Instead, I look forward to my time cooking as a calming and heartwarming experience. I have endless memories of being in the kitchen with my mom, watching her whip up one of her magical meals. With a few sparse ingredients she could create an amazing feast. My dad would bring in some fresh vegetables from our garden, and she would turn them into the most delicious thing I had ever eaten.

As you might imagine, my mother quickly developed the well-deserved reputation for being the best cook in the neighborhood. On any given day there was at least one friend staying over for dinner, often a small army! It was years before I realized that not *every* mother was as great a cook as mine, nor had the love of food and generosity of spirit to literally feed an entire neighborhood.

I didn't realize how fortunate I was to have such a big, loving family to teach me the beauty of respecting the food we put in to our bodies. When I moved to New York City in my late teens to attend New York University and intern at MTV, I was no longer eating the way I had been taught as a child. The days of well-balanced family meals disappeared, and they were replaced with a standard "American" diet of takeout and deli food. It was cheap, and it was convenient. What wasn't convenient was my expanding

To Greeks, food is not just food.
It represents love. It represents family.

waistline and my distressed skin. Although I was eating less food, I was gaining weight. That's when I realized the nutrient-dense, whole food diet on which I was raised was not only full of love but was clearly much better for my body and well-being.

Feeding us a traditional Mediterranean diet wasn't a conscious effort on my mother's part to start my family on a health kick. It was simply the diet and lifestyle she was raised on. It's just how we Greeks eat and have eaten for centuries. A classic Mediterranean diet is rich in fresh organic, seasonally available and locally grown fruits and vegetables, extra-virgin olive oil, oregano, parsley, lemon, and organic, free-range, and hormone-free meat, poultry, and seafood. Consciously or not, my mother was ahead of her time. I strongly believe this is the way we humans were intended to eat.

As you will no doubt see as you begin to cook from this book, Greek dishes are made with whole, natural ingredients from the earth. In Greece, vegetables are almost always organic because most Greek farmers would *never* consider using pesticides on something that they would put into their own bodies, much less bring to market for others to consume. It is just common sense to them. Fruits and vegetables

are picked at the peak of ripeness, and they are on your lunch table that same afternoon. The same rules apply for their poultry, livestock, and fish. Animals are treated incredibly humanely and roam free on farms (or in people's gardens), and when another living creature gives its life to nourish us, that creature is honored and never taken for granted. Every part of it is used for some form of sustenance. The eggs, the milk, the wool, the meat, the bones, and even the skins. Nothing is wasted, for that is considered sinful.

Ironically, the word *organic* has little meaning to Greeks. When people started to become more aware of what goes into the foods we eat here in America, and the word *organic* was suddenly everywhere, my mom was baffled. She said, "*Organic*? What is this, honey? Oh, they mean normal and natural. The way God intended." To her, growing up in Greece, *organic* was all they ever had.

When I reflect on my "Greekness" and what it means to me, the thing I love most about my culture is how warm and welcoming we are. Greeks love to generously share their love of food and their love of life with everyone. There is a word in the Greek language, *philotimo*, which has no equivalent translation in the English language or any other language for that matter. Its literal translation is "friend of honor" or "love of honor," but those phrases cannot define the true depth and complexity of this seemingly simple word. *Philotimo* is a powerful concept. It is a way of being in the world and relating to others that all Greeks learn from a very early age. *Philotimo* is considered the highest of virtues in Greece, and it is something in which we Greeks take much pride. It is about doing what is right, not just what is convenient and right for *you* but what is right for the universal order of things. Your *philotimo* is a badge of honor that shows the world what kind of person you are and what kind of character you have. Every family in Greece instills this concept in their children.

Philotimo embodies an array of crucial values. It is about the unconditional love of family and friends, performing random acts of kindness, and never expecting anything in return. In Greece, all of these virtues are practiced on a regular basis. You see, Greeks don't practice *philotimo* to try to impress others. They do it because it feels right to treat the world we live in and our fellow man with respect. *Philotimo* is about expressing total gratitude for life. It is about paying it forward. It is one of the core, rock-solid values that all Greeks posses. The ancient Greek philosopher Thales (c. 624 BC–c. 546 BC), who Aristotle considered Greece's first philosopher, wrote, "*Philotimo* to the Greek is like breathing. A Greek is not a Greek without it. He might as well not be alive."

Personally, I am honored and humbled to be part of such a rich culture. And like so many Greeks before me, I want to share my culture with the world so that everyone can experience the love and the *philotimo* I have felt throughout my life. My first step in doing so is to share my family's century-old recipes with everyone (much to the chagrin of my sister Maria, who was holding on to her *baklava* recipe for dear life. Sorry Maria! The secret's out!). I wanted to show the world that Greek food is not just *gyro*, *souvlaki*, and Greek yogurt. Although those are all pretty yummy, there is a lot more to traditional Greek cuisine. The recipes in this book will prove it. These are recipes that have been passed down in my family for generations. They are both scrumptious and great for you. And they are all made with love. My hope is to make my family proud by sharing their treasured recipes with you so that you too can enjoy them with your friends and family. Let us all share in the *philotimo* of Greece together. *Opa!!*

Stin igieia sou kai kali orexi,
(To your health and good appetite,)

—Debbie Matenopoulos

This *Is Greece!*

I used to watch Debbie on the *The View* when I was in college. On Mondays and Wednesdays, after my early morning classes, I would go back to my dorm room and switch on the TV. I remember thinking, "Who is this girl, and who had the balls to put her on live network television next to Barbara Walters?!" Just as she does now, Debbie had an infectious free spirit, and she was totally fearless, even in her early twenties sitting next to the likes of Barbara Walters and Meredith Vieira. She made a huge impression on me back then, even though at the time I had no idea our paths would ever cross.

A few years after college, I landed a job working as a producer on a new show for E! News. Debbie was brought on as one of the hosts, and I remember the moment she walked through the door for our first meeting. She sat right next to me, and we became fast friends. You see, Debbie has a way of lighting up a room when she enters. Her smile makes you feel like you can literally do anything. She has incredible empathy, a way of relating to people that is both engaging and empowering. Those are the reasons she is great on television, and those are the reasons I loved her as a friend from the moment I met her.

For Debbie, I learned quickly, food and family have always gone hand in hand. I remember being so moved and excited when she invited me over to her house for Thanksgiving. We hadn't known each other for that long, yet she knew that I was a recent transplant to Los Angeles from New York. And so without thinking twice, she took me in with so many of her friends for her "Orphans' Thanksgiving." I will never forget the image of Debbie triumphantly lifting a 30-pound turkey in a huge roasting pan out of the oven, by herself, and setting it down on her kitchen island. Pretty much all on her own, she cooked a huge, amazing meal for a big group of us, and it was clear that she found genuine pleasure in watching everyone enjoying the food she had prepared and each other's company.

This past year, Debbie and I decided to work together on developing a couple of TV projects. It was during the development process that she began to share with me just how extensive her culinary background was. One day she showed up to a writing session with a couple of very old notebooks, all in Greek, crammed full of authentic recipes. I asked her how many recipes she had, and she told me that among her, her mom, her aunt, and her extended Greek family, she probably had more than five hundred. My jaw dropped, and I knew we had to do a book. Luckily Glenn at BenBella agreed with me, and thus began a whirlwind process of writing and photographing.

Before I had a chance to blink, Debbie, our incredible photographer Jon Falcone, and I had landed in Greece. My type-A personality was in high gear trying to figure out how we were going to get done all that we had to do in the short time we had to do it. But Greece, you see, already had plans for me, plans for *us*. On our second day in Athens, I asked our good friend and enlisted guide Yanni to take me to the local Vodafone so that I could buy a prepaid SIM card for my iPad, as I had done on trips all around the world. As I walked into the store, a salesman greeted me, casually smoking a cigarette, and informed me, "This is Greece. It's August. We don't have cards." When I protested, explaining to him that he only sold three things—phones, tablets, and the cards to make the phones and tablets work—he nodded as if to thank me for enlightening him as to the nature of what he does every day and reiterated, "This is Greece. It's August. We don't have cards." Again I protested, this time insisting that he call another Vodafone store, which he did graciously. He carried on a lengthy conversation in Greek over the phone, laughing and enjoying himself for what seemed like ten minutes. Upon hanging up the phone, his smile faded as his eyes met mine, and again he said, "This is Greece. It's August. *He* don't have cards." He went on to explain to me that in Greece, in August, everyone goes on vacation, and everything in the whole country grinds to a halt.

With renewed TV producer determination and a distinctly furrowed brow, I returned to the car, where a knowing Yanni was waiting. He began to laugh when he saw my face and exclaimed, "This is *GREECE*, my friend!" At which point I rolled my eyes and pleaded with him to

take me to the Cosmote, the Greek version of AT&T. Two Cosmote stores and an hour later, we returned to Yanni's apartment with no SIM card. Debbie saw my scrunched-up face and started laughing. "Peter! Relax! This is Greece!"

Jon, our photographer, looked at Debbie and pondered, "Why does everyone keep saying that here? We know where we are."

"Because this is Greece!" was the only answer that would ever be forthcoming, and ultimately the only answer that would make any sense.

Greece, I would learn, is not just a country but a way of life. It is an ancient culture steeped in tradition and steadfast in its belief in the power of the universe to take care of everything in life. The infectious faith of the Greek people was, for me, totally magical. Because of this unshakable faith in the grace and goodness of the Infinite, I quickly realized that Greece is a place where the "common sense" we learn in America simply does not apply. The people of Greece so strongly believe that they will be taken care of that their lives lack the stress and anxiety that we Americans so happily claim as our birthright. Greece is a place where God exists everywhere and in everything, and where prayers are both heard and answered. Beyond their faith in the divine, the Greek people are deeply in touch with the earth and the seasons, and they live breath to breath, moment to moment, and day to day. I never met anyone there who would dream of letting the idea of tomorrow rob them of the joy of today. Food and family are paramount, and anything that would dare come between them has no place in anyone's life. It's as simple as that.

One day, early on in our trip, Jon and I were frantically chasing the sunlight as we tried to set up shot after shot of the food in this book. Debbie's mom and aunt were working better, faster, and harder than any professional chefs or food stylists I have ever met. As they cranked out dish after dish made completely from scratch, Jon shot photo after photo. When

we were done photographing any particular dish, I would return it to the kitchen table and inform everyone that they could now begin to eat it. As the afternoon dragged on, I noticed that more and more of Debbie's family members were arriving, and yet none of the food had been touched. Everyone was just sitting in the living room, staring at the food and then looking back at me like I was absolutely insane.

Thinking I was being polite, I offered, "Please don't wait for us! Start eating!" All I got in return were more bewildered stares and silence. Finally, Debbie emerged from the house, looking defeated. She said, "You have to stop. I don't care about the light. I don't care about the schedule. You have to stop. You don't understand. Right now you and Jon are being rude and offensive."

I was stunned. I have been called a lot of things in my life, but "rude and offensive" were never words that were thrown my way. And what was harder for me to accept than having unintentionally offended Debbie's family was that I had no idea what I had done and, therefore, no idea how I could begin to make amends. It turned out what I had done was quite simple. I had ignored one of the most sacred experiences of life in Greece: the taking of time to break bread in the afternoon with friends and family. Greek people don't graze. They don't grab plates and eat buffet style sitting in the living room or standing up wherever they can find space. Like Thanksgiving in America, the afternoon meal in Greece is served at the table, and the whole group of family and friends gathers, sits down, enjoys the blessings of the food together, and then rests. Unintentionally or not, Jon and I had violated one of the most important customs in all of Greece.

After that day, we quickly learned to schedule our work around the family in Greece. And slowly, albeit unconsciously, Jon and I began to trust in the universe to take care of it. We began to believe that everything would just work out because everyone and everything around us told us so. In my case, I began to feel amazing. I felt the stress and anxiety leave my body, slowly, day by day. I felt healthier than I had ever felt in my life, eating farm-fresh food and taking the time to enjoy the whole experience of life. I began to understand what made Debbie, well, Debbie. I learned more about how to live a good life from Debbie and her family and the Greek culture on our relatively brief trip than I have in any other experience in my life so far. I have never felt better in my life than I did in Greece. And, as a side note, when I returned home, my housekeeper, Carmen, asked me where I had been. "You look at least three years younger!" she exclaimed. I think she thought I'd had Botox injections.

Oh, and that iPad SIM card? We never did get one, and we actually never needed it. Greece took care of everything because *that* is Greece.

—Peter Capozzi

How to Use This Book

In modern Greece, people still live in the spirit of the ancient Greek philosophy inscribed on the Temple of Apollo at Delphi: μηδὲν ἄγαν (*mithen agan*), which means "nothing in excess." One of the main reasons the Greek people are so healthy and live such long and vital lives is that while they certainly allow themselves the occasional pleasure of very rich foods and desserts, they balance those indulgences with hearty servings of salads and vegetables. In fact, in Greece, people "fast" seasonally, which means they engage in a vegan diet as a means of worship and cleansing. These fasting periods allow the Greeks to rebalance themselves in body, mind, and spirit.

It is in *this* spirit that we proudly present the recipes in this book. In Greece, a small serving of *moussaka* or *pastichio* would occupy no more than one-quarter of a standard dinner plate. The rest of the plate would be filled with a variety of fresh, seasonally available vegetables and salads. Additionally, the afternoon meal in Greece is what we in America would consider dinner. It is the largest meal of the day and is almost always enjoyed together with family and friends. Afterward, there is a siesta period, where people have an opportunity to rest so that they can digest their meals and rejoin their day refreshed and renewed.

The Greek evening meal is essentially a small supper. A satisfying bowl of soup and a healthy serving of salad accompanied by a thick slice of crusty bread is a perfect example of what a

The afternoon meal in Greece is what we in America would consider dinner. It is the largest meal of the day and is almost always enjoyed together with family and friends.

typical Greek family would enjoy together as the last meal of the day. By not retiring for the night with an overly full stomach, Greeks tend to sleep easier and more restfully

In Greece, sweet pastries and cookies are not traditionally served after a large meal. Instead, a large plate or bowl of fresh fruit is served family style at the table. What Americans consider *dessert*—cakes, cookies, and other sweet pastries—are usually enjoyed in small servings, at midday, with a small cup of Greek coffee, as a snack for guests, or in town with friends at a local bakery or sweet shop. Larger servings would be enjoyed and shared among friends and family.

As you begin to enjoy these recipes, initially you may find that the food tastes undersalted. In Greece, salt is used to enhance the deep and natural flavors of the food rather than to become the flavor of the food itself, as is so often the case in American cuisine. Taste each finished dish and adjust seasoning as desired.

Buying locally decreases the distance food must travel between farm and table, which allows for fresher, more flavorful food.

quick-to-prepare salads. Allow those salads and vegetables to occupy about 75 percent of the plate. Serve seasonally available fruit after meals, and savor cakes, cookies, and pastries occasionally at midday and with friends and family. Try to have your largest meal of the day at lunchtime, and reserve evenings for light and nourishing suppers.

As a final note, many of the dishes in this book are vegan or can be prepared that way. Vegan food can be absolutely delicious and satisfying, and the recipes in this book will not disappoint. Preparing completely plant-based meals a few times a week for you and your family and friends can make a huge difference for your health and the health of your loved ones.

Of course, these ideas are simply our opinion based on our own personal experience. Before making any major lifestyle and/or diet changes, always consult a qualified professional to determine the right course of action.

We wish you great health and abundance as you enjoy this book. *Stin ighia sou!*

The recipes in this book are designed to allow the essence of the ingredients to shine through. To that end, we recommend that you choose the ripest, freshest organic produce you can find. When choosing meats, poultry, and fish, look for organic, free range, and sustainably raised. Buying locally decreases the distance food must travel between farm and table, which allows for fresher, more flavorful food, not to mention greatly reduces our carbon footprint.

We encourage you to follow these guidelines as you and your family plan your own meals from the recipes in this book. Enjoy rich dishes in moderation with a variety of vegetables and

A Few Cooking Tips

QUICK-SOAK METHOD FOR BEANS

If you do not have time to soak beans overnight, do not fret. The quick-soak method works just as well. Pick over and rinse dried beans very well. Transfer the beans to a large stockpot, and cover them with 3 inches of cold water. Set the pot over medium-high heat, and bring to a boil, uncovered. Boil for 3 minutes, remove from the heat, cover, and let the beans sit in the hot water for 1 hour. After 1 hour, drain the beans, rinse well, and proceed with the recipe.

BAKING

When baking, assume that your oven has uneven heat and hot spots. Thus, to ensure even and consistent baking, rotate all baking dishes and pans 180 degrees halfway through baking.

PEELING AND SEEDING TOMATOES

The easiest way to peel tomatoes is to use a paring knife to cut out the core at the top and then score an ✕ through the skin at the bottom. Lower the tomatoes into a pot of boiling water for 1 minute. Using a slotted spoon, remove the tomatoes and quickly dunk them into a bowl of ice water for 30 seconds to stop the cooking. Begin peeling at the bottom where the tomatoes were scored. The skins should slip off very easily. (This method is also used to peel peaches.)

To seed tomatoes, gently squeeze the whole peeled tomato over the sink. The seeds will pop right out, and you can rinse them away. Then slice the tomato flesh and proceed with the recipe.

PREPARING VEGETABLES FOR COOKING

Recipes in this book are written with the assumption that vegetables and fruits are to be washed well before cooking. Carrots and other root vegetables should be scrubbed well, and peeled when specified in the recipe. Garlic should be peeled by smashing each clove with the flat side of a knife, which makes the skins easy to slip off.

Leeks are grown in sandy soil; you must wash them carefully so that your finished dish won't be gritty. Run whole leeks under cold water to wash away visible dirt, then cut off the roots and trim the tough dark green parts (the top 2 to 4 inches) away from the tops. (Don't waste vegetable trimmings; save them for the next time you make stock.) Cut the leeks lengthwise in half, and slice as the recipe directs. Submerge the slices in a bowl of cold water. Use your hands to swish them around, then lift them out and drain well.

RICE

Some cooks rinse their rice, while others do not. Arborio rice and enriched rice should never be rinsed. Rinsing rice removes some of the starches, as well as any impurities, and creates a fluffier, separate grain when cooked, but this process can also rinse away some of the nutrients. Where rinsing is essential to ensure the outcome of a particular recipe, we've included it in the steps. Otherwise, we leave it up to you.

The Greek Pantry: From Alpha to Omega (A–Ω)

A strategically stocked pantry is crucial for all home cooks. With only a few of the items listed next, just about anyone could whip up a feast fit for a Greek god. Many of these staples are important to all kitchens while others are more esoteric and specific to the Greek kitchen. The following pages will help you to better understand how to select the very best ingredients for your own kitchen and guide you through the recipes in this book.

BREAD CRUMBS. Always use plain, unseasoned bread crumbs for the recipes in this book. You will have far more control over the final outcome of your dish when you are in control of the amount of salt and seasonings in all the ingredients. You can easily make your own bread crumbs by slicing up some day-old bread and leaving it out overnight, allowing it to dry out. The next day, toss it in a food processor or high-performance blender and pulse until the desired consistency is reached.

BUTTER, DAIRY. With the exception of the butter used to make the savory phyllo *pites*, all butter mentioned in this book is unsalted. Choosing unsalted butter allows you to control exactly how much salt is used in any given dish. Debbie's mom always uses Land O'Lakes butter (both salted and unsalted), so we recommend choosing that brand whenever possible. Land O'Lakes is noted among professional chefs and bakers alike for its superior flavor and consistency.

BUTTER, VEGAN. A few of the sweet pastries in this book can be made vegan simply by using a vegan butter substitute in place of the butter. We recommend Earth Balance Vegan Buttery Sticks for their consistency and ease of use. Regardless of which vegan butter substitute you choose, always make sure you use one without hydrogenated oils.

CAPERS. Capers are sold in jars packed in brine or salt. Both varieties are delicious and can be used interchangeably for the recipes in this book. Regardless of which kind you choose, be sure to rinse the capers well before using.

CINNAMON. In some regions of Greece, cinnamon is used prolifically in both sweet and savory dishes. Keep both pure ground cinnamon (not cinnamon sugar) and cinnamon sticks in your spice cabinet. While cinnamon is a very pleasantly scented spice, it is also extremely pungent, so use it sparingly. Ground cinnamon loses its strength over time, so be sure your supply is fresh. Cinnamon has many health benefits: It is believed to balance blood sugar, boost the immune system, prevent blood clots, relieve indigestion, and reduce the negative impact of high-fat meals.

CUMIN. Cumin is a lovely earthy spice, and it gives a very characteristic flavor to many hearty dishes. It is used to provide warmth to beans and lentils as well as to meats and poultry. Ground cumin is available in most markets. If you are truly adventurous, you can buy cumin seeds, toast them yourself, and then grind them for use. All of the recipes in this book refer to ground cumin. A little goes a long way!

DILL. Along with parsley and dried oregano, dill is one of the most frequently used herbs in all of Greek cuisine. Its refreshing aromatic flavor is instantly recognizable, and it can't even be up-staged by copious amounts of garlic in *tzatziki*. Always opt for fresh dill whenever possible.

EGGS. Use organic Grade A large eggs for best results.

EXTRA-VIRGIN OLIVE OIL. "Extra-virgin" refers to the first cold pressing of perfectly ripe olives and is characterized by its low acidity and delicious flavor. Obviously, we prefer Greek olive oil to any other. But if you can't find Greek olive oil at your local market, there are many other wonderful varieties from Italy, Spain, and even California. Some olive oils have a stronger flavor than others. Experiment and find a few you like. Oils with a deeper color usually have more in-tense flavor; however, be discerning. Some producers use additives to color their oils in order to fool consumers. Choose an extra-virgin olive oil with a flavor you and your family enjoy. Store it in a cool, dark place but do not refrigerate.

FETA. Feta has gotten a bad rap in America due to the abundance of poorly produced, overly pungent, waxy cheese that unfortunately has been called feta. A truly delicious feta is made from sheep's or goat's milk, should be satisfy-ingly salty, and has a mouth feel that is both moist and pleasingly smooth. Though feta is a relatively hard cheese, good-quality feta is never dry and has a velvety unctuousness to it. For the recipes in this book, the best feta cheese is likely sourced from Greece or Bulgaria. When possible, choose brine-packed feta purchased at the cheese or deli counter of your favorite gour-met market rather than a prepackaged variety. Barrel-aged feta (also in brine) has the most velvety and creamy quality of all. When buying feta, ask that it be packed in its brine rather than packaged dry. Feta lasts longer in its brine. In Greece, a thick slice of feta is served for the table at nearly every meal, drizzled with olive oil and seasoned with dried oregano. My personal man-tra is, "Life is *betta* with feta."

GARLIC. What can be written about garlic that has not already been written? You either love it or you hate it, but there is no denying its abundant use in all of Mediterranean cuisine. It has been used by humans for over seven thousand years

as both food and medicine, and it serves both purposes today. Choose the freshest garlic heads you can find. They should feel heavy and dense for their size, a sure sign the cloves are plump and juicy. Avoid heads sprouting with green shoots.

GIGANTES. *Gigantes* are giant white beans, sold dry in packages, similar to large cannellini beans. Rich and satisfying, they keep indefinitely in the cupboard in an airtight container. Preparing them takes some time, but they are well worth the effort. You will find them online or in Greek and Mediterranean specialty shops.

GREEK YOGURT. Hearty yet refreshing and light at the same time, Greek yogurt is thicker than the typical store-bought yogurt so many Americans are used to. Its thickness comes from the fact that it is strained of extraneous liquid prior to packaging. In our opinion, it's the best yogurt in the world. Add some local honey (or, better yet, Greek honey if you can find it), and be prepared for your taste buds to cry, "*Opa!*"

HONEY. In Greece, honey is literally known as the nectar of the gods. Greek honey is unparalleled anywhere in the world. The abundant varieties of plants, herbs, and flowers throughout Greece create a rich environment for honeybees to do their best work. My two favorite brands of Greek honey are Attiki and Monastiri, which can be found in many markets across America.

If you cannot find Greek honey, it is always fun to seek out the honey purveyors at your local farmers' market. The closest thing to Greek honey is thyme blossom honey, which is truly delicious. Try out other less common locally available honeys to find your favorite. Many studies have indicated that honey can be used effectively in the fight against cancer. For medicinal use, honey has antifungal, antiviral, and antibacterial properties.

HORTA (DANDELION GREENS). One man's trash is another man's treasure! For years people have battled to rid their lawns of this so-called pesky weed. Little did they know just how delicious and nutritious these robust greens really are. With a flavor reminiscent of arugula and a texture similar to collard greens, *horta* are high in calcium, rich in iron, powerful anti-inflammatory agents, and believed to provide a thorough liver cleanse. Vegans take note: They also have more protein per serving than spinach and contain all the essential amino acids. In other words, if you are not eating these supergreens regularly, you should be!

KALAMATA OLIVES. Kalamata olives are the most famous of the Greek olives, both within Greece and around the world. These salty, delicious, eggplant-color, meaty olives hail from the Kalamata region of Greece. Although dozens of varieties of olives are grown throughout Greece, for the purposes of this book, we refer only to Kalamata olives, as they are the most readily available in America. They are sold in jars in the olives section of most markets, or you can find them fresh from the barrel and straight from Greece in both Mediterranean and specialty gourmet food shops.

KEFALOTIRI. Kefalotiri is a hard cheese, typically sliced or grated. It can be used like Parmesan cheese, grated over or into many Greek dishes. It is also traditionally served as an appetizer with olives and ice-cold ouzo. A salty sheep's and/or goat's milk cheese, kefalotiri is the more intense Greek cousin of Gruyère and has a flavor profile somewhere in between Gruyère and Parmesan.

LEEKS. Leeks are a member of the onion family, but they are really what onions wish they were. If an onion died and went to heaven, it would become a leek. In America, leeks tend to be underrated. They have an amazing and unique flavor that is both sweet and savory while also being pleasantly mild. Greeks use leeks as a main ingredient for fillings in phyllo *pites* as well as a key component in many meat dishes. Although they can be a little daunting to prepare, they are certainly worth the effort. Many markets today sell cleaned and sliced leeks, so don't be intimidated if you've never used them before.

LEMONS. Every self-respecting Greek cook has a kitchen well stocked with fresh lemons. Lemon juice is a fantastic flavor enhancer, and it is also a perfect partner with olive oil. Believe it or not, a tiny squeeze of lemon juice can really amp up the flavor of your favorite dishes. Lemons are used throughout Mediterranean cuisine to brighten meats, fish, poultry, vegetables, and even desserts. Always squeeze your own fresh lemon juice; never use bottled.

LENTILS. Lentils are wonderful. Incredibly rich in iron and packed with both protein and fiber, they keep for months and months, and we recommend that you keep some around to whip up a quick soup or salad. They are quick cooking and easy to prepare. As they come in a variety of sizes and colors, we encourage you to experiment and find what you and your family like. We prefer the brown variety because they are universally available. Store lentils in the pantry in an airtight container.

MINT. Fresh mint is fantastic! Not only is it a great digestive, but it adds a superb cooling freshness to whatever dish it is used to enhance. In Greece, the interesting flavor of mint is used in both sweet and savory dishes. It is found in nearly every Greek garden, and you'll find its refreshing aroma wafting through most Greek homes. Be mindful, though—a little mint goes a very long way!

OIL FOR FRYING. Many of the recipes in this book include vegetable or olive oil for deep or pan frying. We do not recommend using extra-virgin olive oil for frying due to its very low smoke point. Instead, we recommend using a neutral-flavor oil that can withstand higher heat. Great options include safflower and canola oil. Be sure to choose only organic, expeller-pressed oils refined for medium- to high-heat cooking. You can also use an olive oil refined for higher-heat cooking, if desired.

ONIONS. The recipes in this book call for yellow, Vidalia, and red onions. We choose organic onions whenever possible. Yellow and Vidalia onions are generally sautéed to add a great base flavor to cooked meat and vegetable dishes. They have a sweet, mild flavor, and they do not overpower the other ingredients. Red onions are often used raw in salads. You can also use these onions interchangeably. Experiment to see which ones you like best.

OREGANO, DRIED. In most cases you would never choose a dried herb over its fresh counterpart, but we do recommend using dried oregano, as fresh oregano tends to be way too overpowering. In Greek cooking, it is rare to find a dish that calls for fresh oregano. With respect to dried oregano, please do your best to find the Greek. In a pinch, you can use Italian, but there really is no comparison. Greek oregano has a characteristic brightness and a bigger flavor than its counterparts.

ORZO. Orzo is the national pasta of Greece. It resembles rice in shape, and when cooked, it looks like rice on steroids. This delicious pasta is a perfect accompaniment to so many of the soups, stews, and main dishes in this book.

PARMESAN CHEESE. For the recipes in this book, we recommend substituting Parmesan for kefalotiri if kefalotiri is unavailable. Choose authentic Parmigiano-Reggiano whenever possible for the most satisfying and rich flavor.

PARSLEY, ITALIAN FLAT-LEAF. This is where the Italians come in! We love their parsley. You would be hard-pressed to find a dish in Greece that does not call for fresh Italian flat-leaf parsley. Sometimes it takes center stage in a recipe, and other times it fades into the background, providing a fresh accent. Either way, it is a staple in Greek cooking. It has a superior flavor to its curly counterpart.

PEPPERCORNS, WHOLE BLACK. If you are serious about your food, we recommend investing in a pepper grinder and whole black peppercorns. Pre-ground pepper quickly loses its pungency and flavor. Whole peppercorns stay fresh for much longer, and there is no substitute for that fresh-cracked pepper taste.

PHYLLO DOUGH. It's almost impossible to think of Greek cuisine without including phyllo dough. This flaky, many-layered dough is used for both savory *pites* and sweet pastries alike. You can make your own thicker, country-style phyllo dough; however, for the purposes of this book, we refer to the thinner, commercially available variety. Always keep a 13 × 18-inch, 1-pound package in your freezer. Thaw phyllo overnight in your refrigerator before using in your favorite recipes.

POTATOES. Potatoes come in many shapes, colors, and sizes. For the purposes of this book, we use russet and Yukon Gold potatoes. Whenever possible, choose organic potatoes.

RICE. The recipes in this book refer to both white and brown rice. We recommend choosing organic, long-grain rice. Brown rice has a distinct nutty flavor and takes a little longer to cook, but its high nutritional profile and wonderful texture make it worth the wait. Packages of rice should be refrigerated or frozen after opening to prolong their life.

SEA SALT. In our kitchen, we prefer to use sea salt, which usually has a milder flavor than a typical table salt. As it comes from the sea, it contains other minerals, which can be beneficial to health and well-being. Many varieties of sea salt are available today. Pick one that you and your family enjoy.

TAHINI. Tahini is a thick, creamy paste made from sesame seeds. Processed similarly to a nut butter, tahini has its own very distinct flavor. It is widely available in grocery and specialty stores alike. Choose organic when available.

TARAMA. Tarama is a type of cured pink fish roe, basically the equivalent of a Greek caviar. Traditionally it is made from carp roe, but over the years, other varieties have become common as well. It is very salty and is used for making *taramosalata*. We recommend the Krinos brand if you can find it. It is widely available in the international section of most markets, online, and in gourmet specialty shops.

TOMATO PASTE. If ever there was a secret ingredient in any cuisine, tomato paste is it for the Greeks. It is made simply by cooking tomatoes for hours until a pastelike consistency is achieved and is sold in cans or tubes. Tomato paste from a can will keep for several weeks when stored in an airtight container in the refrigerator. If you only use small amounts at a time, a tube is a great choice, as you can squeeze out only the amount you need. The flavor is very intense and really amps up any dish to which it is added. It provides a depth and richness that tomatoes, fresh or canned, alone simply cannot provide. A tablespoon or two can really be a game changer.

TOMATOES. Like garlic, lemons, and parsley, tomatoes are front and center in every Greek kitchen. Used in soups, sauces, salads, and even eaten stuffed, tomatoes are hearty, resilient, and delicious. Research suggests tomatoes support bone strength and health, provide cardiovascular support, reduce inflammation, and have cancer-prevention potential. Many varieties of tomatoes are available today. Always buy organic whenever possible, and choose the ripest tomatoes you can find for the richest flavor. Your best bet is to buy your tomatoes at your local farm market in season and use high-quality, organic canned tomatoes when fresh, local ones are not available. Tomatoes lose their flavor quickly when refrigerated, so store them at room temperature.

VANILLA EXTRACT. Not all vanilla extracts are created equal. Choose a very high quality, pure bourbon vanilla extract, and do not be fooled by anything labeled "imitation."

VINEGAR. As well as being a fantastic flavor enhancer, vinegar is both a digestive and a preservative. Greeks use it for so many purposes in the kitchen. For the recipes in this book, we use only white wine, red wine, and apple cider vinegars. Balsamic vinegar is not used in traditional Greek cooking. Very good quality red and white wine vinegars are worth the investment; as with wine, you will likely wince when you taste a substandard vinegar. We recommend choosing a raw and organic apple cider vinegar, still containing "the mother."

ACROPOLIS

The most famous landmark in all of Greece is undoubtedly the Acropolis in Athens. *Acro* translates to "edge," and *polis* translates to "city," so *Acropolis* literally means "the edge of the city." The name *Acropolis* refers to the high rocky outcropping on top of which sits what is arguably the most famous structure in all of Greece, the Parthenon. The Parthenon is a vital symbol of the Greek legacy and a truc remembrance

of classical Greece. The Acropolis is comprised of two large amphitheaters and a number of other structures of great historical significance. Standing on the ancient ruins of this immense stone citadel, which is believed to have been first inhabited in the fourth millennium BC, has always given me great pride in the contributions of my Greek ancestors to this world. However, basking in the glory of their incredible creation high above the city of Athens, I cannot help but also feel a little insignificant in the grand scheme of things! It was very important for me to include a tribute to this magnificent monument in this book. And in our attempt to do so, we ended up being locked in, detained for questioning, and nearly arrested. All in a day's work!

Mezzethes
APPETIZERS

Mezzethes are small to medium plates of appetizers that are served family style. Like tapas in Spanish cuisine, *mezzethes* are often the main attraction at a Greek meal. It's fun and easy to create an entire meal comprised only of *mezzethes*. They are almost always served with *Tzatziki* (page 76), *Horiatki Salata* (traditional Greek salad, page 86), freshly baked bread or oven-warmed pita, and ice-cold Retsina (Greek table wine) or ouzo. The recipes in this chapter serve 4 to 6 people, but they're easily doubled to accommodate a larger crowd. Try serving *mezzethes* in place of your typical party snacks or appetizers at your next gathering.

Croquettes Patatas (kro-KEH-tes pah-tah-TES)

POTATO CROQUETTES

Croquettes Patatas are essentially the Greek answer to the Tater Tot, but these light, crunchy bites of seasoned potato are far superior to anything my elementary school lunch lady ever served me. Cook up a batch for a family treat or a fun gathering. No ketchup required!

SERVES 4 TO 6

1 pound russet potatoes, unpeeled
4 large eggs, separated
½ cup grated kefalotiri *or* Parmesan cheese
1 teaspoon sea salt
¼ teaspoon freshly ground black pepper
½ cup finely chopped onion
3 tablespoons finely chopped fresh Italian
    flat-leaf parsley
2 tablespoons water
1½ cups unseasoned dry bread crumbs
Olive or vegetable oil, for frying

Preheat oven to 250 degrees.

Boil the potatoes in their skins for 25 to 30 minutes or until soft. Drain and set aside until cool enough to handle. Peel the potatoes and mash them well in a large mixing bowl. Add the egg yolks, kefalotiri or Parmesan cheese, salt, pepper, onion, and parsley, and mix well until all ingredients are incorporated.

In a medium mixing bowl, beat the egg whites together with the water until well mixed and a little fluffy.

Line a large baking dish or rimmed baking sheet with unbleached parchment paper. Using a tablespoon as a measure, scoop out the dough and roll it into a meatball shape. Dip the croquette in the bread crumbs, then into the egg whites, then into the bread crumbs again. Place the croquette on the prepared pan, and continue in this manner until you have used up all the dough.

In a large, deep skillet or pot set over medium heat, heat ½ inch of the oil until it shimmers. Working in batches, carefully add a few croquettes at a time to the hot oil. Using a metal spatula, gently flatten the croquettes into ½-inch-thick patties. Cook until golden, about 4 to 5 minutes per side. Remove the finished croquettes to an oven-safe platter lined with paper towels to drain. Keep the cooked croquettes warm in the oven until all have been fried. Serve immediately.

YIAYIA'S TIP: When heating oil for pan frying, watch it carefully, and don't allow it to smoke, as this will affect the flavor of your food. Your oil is ready when the surface begins to shimmer. Different oils have different smoke points, so keep an eye on the pan, and don't leave it unattended.

Souvlaki Psaro me Latholemono

(soo-VLAH-kee psa-ROH meh lah-thoh-leh-moh-NOH)

LEMON–OLIVE OIL MARINATED FISH KEBABS

Shish kebabs are fun to make and serve, and these *fish* kebabs are a lighter variation on the classic. Timeless and totally tasty, they are easy to assemble, easy to grill, and fun to eat.

SERVES 8

1 recipe *Latholemono* (page 73)

2 cloves garlic, finely chopped

½ teaspoon dried oregano

1½ pounds thick whitefish fillets (like halibut, grouper, or cod), cut into roughly 40 (1½-inch) cubes

8 shish kebab sticks, soaked in water at least 20 minutes (if wooden) to prevent burning

2 medium red bell peppers, washed, seeded, and cut into 1½-inch squares

2 medium green peppers, washed, seeded, and cut into 1½-inch squares

3 tablespoons olive oil (to brush the grill)

Whisk the *Latholemono* with the garlic and oregano in a large mixing bowl. Add the fish and gently toss with the dressing, taking care not to break up the fish. Cover and refrigerate for 1 hour to marinate.

Prepare the grill by setting a gas grill to high or preparing a very hot charcoal fire.

To assemble the kebabs, skewer 1 piece of fish, followed by 1 piece of red or green pepper, another piece of fish, 1 piece of pepper of the alternate color, and so on, until you have about 5 pieces of fish on each kebab. Lightly brush the grill with the olive oil to prevent sticking and grill the kebabs for 6 to 8 minutes total, turning a quarter turn every 1½ to 2 minutes. Serve immediately.

VARIATION: To bake the kebabs, preheat oven to 350 degrees. Place assembled kebabs on a large baking sheet lined with unbleached parchment paper. Bake for about 15 minutes or until the peppers are tender and the fish is cooked through. Rotate the kebabs once while cooking, and lightly brush them with a little more *Latholemono* if they get too dry. Serve immediately.

———————— 🇬🇷 ————————

DEBBIE'S TIP: To serve as a main course, allow 2 kebabs per person. Serve with *Pilafi* (page 230), *Horiatki Salata* (page 86), or a simple side dish or salad of your choosing.

Dolmathes Gyalantzi *(DOHL-mah-thes Yah-lan-ZEE)*

STUFFED GRAPE LEAVES

Who doesn't love stuffed grape leaves? These are probably one of the most recognizable Greek *mezzethes,* and they are certainly on my list of all-time favorites. They are equally delicious hot or cold, so they are a great make-ahead item for any party.

SERVES 8 TO 10

2 16-ounce jars grape leaves

1½ cups extra-virgin olive oil, divided

3 large yellow onions, finely chopped

1½ cups long-grain white rice

2 cups water

1 bunch scallions, white and soft green parts, thinly sliced

½ cup finely chopped fresh Italian flat-leaf parsley

2 tablespoons finely chopped fresh dill

1½ teaspoons finely chopped fresh mint

2¼ teaspoons sea salt, divided

1¼ teaspoons freshly ground black pepper, divided

2 to 3 tablespoons freshly squeezed lemon juice (1 lemon)

Bring a large pot of water to a boil over high heat.

Rinse the grape leaves very well in a colander and drain. Trim any rough edges. Carefully submerge the grape leaves in the boiling water and cook for 3 minutes. Use a fine mesh strainer or slotted spoon to return the grape leaves to the colander, rinse with cold water to stop the cooking, and set aside.

Add ¼ cup of the olive oil to another large pot and set over medium heat. Add the onions and sauté until translucent but not brown, about 5 to 6 minutes, stirring frequently. Add the rice and cook, stirring constantly, until it becomes opaque, about 2 minutes. Add water, scallions, parsley, dill, mint, 2 teaspoons of the salt, and 1 teaspoon of the pepper. Reduce heat to a simmer and cook, stirring constantly to keep from sticking, until the water is absorbed and the rice is tender. Remove from heat and set aside to cool slightly.

Take a grape leaf in the palm of your hand, shiny side down. Place 1 tablespoon of the rice mixture at one end of the leaf. Fold in the outer edges and roll up like a small egg roll, being careful not to tear the leaf. Set filled grape leaves on a large plate. Continue this process until you are out of filling.

Line the bottom of a large pot with the remaining grape leaves. Arrange the stuffed and rolled *dolmathes* in an even layer, seam side down, stacking multiple layers if necessary. Pour the remaining 1¼ cups of olive oil over the stuffed grape leaves and season with the remaining salt and pepper. Gently lay a clean, heatproof plate on top of the grape leaves inside the pot. (The plate should fit inside the pot but be large enough to cover all the leaves.) Add enough warm water (not hot, not cold) to cover the stuffed grape leaves and the plate. Add the lemon juice and put a lid on the pot. Cook over low heat for 30 minutes or until the liquid has evaporated completely. Serve warm or cold.

Psarokeftethes *(psa-roh-kef-TEH-thes)*

FISH CAKES IN TOMATO SAUCE

Like so many classic Greek recipes, these fish cakes grew out of the strong belief that food should never be wasted, especially when another living creature has given its life to nourish you. *Psarokeftethes* can be made with one fish or a variety of different fish, which gives them a truly unique flavor every time you make them. Whatever fish you have on hand will work!

SERVES 4 TO 6

1 pound skinless, boneless whitefish fillet (such as flounder, cod, or grouper)

1¼ teaspoons sea salt, divided

1 cup day-old bread, crusts removed, cut into ½-inch cubes (about 1 to 2 slices)

1 medium yellow onion, grated, excess liquid squeezed out and discarded

3 cloves garlic, finely chopped

½ cup chopped fresh Italian flat-leaf parsley

¼ cup finely chopped fresh mint

¼ cup finely chopped fresh dill

3 tablespoons all-purpose flour

2 tablespoons freshly squeezed lemon juice (1 lemon)

2 large eggs, lightly beaten

¼ teaspoon freshly ground black pepper

Olive or vegetable oil for frying

1 lemon cut into wedges

1 recipe *Tzatziki* (page 76) (optional)

2 cups (½ recipe) *Mama's Domata Saltsa* (page 74) *or* other tomato sauce (optional)

Preheat oven to 350 degrees. Lightly oil a baking dish large enough to hold the fish in a single layer. Season the fish with ½ teaspoon of the salt. Place the fish in the prepared baking dish and bake, uncovered, for 12 to 15 minutes or until cooked through. Remove the fish from the oven and set aside to cool slightly. Reduce oven temperature to 250 degrees.

To make the fish cakes, soak the bread briefly in a bowl of water until wet all the way the through. Squeeze the bread cubes to remove excess water and transfer to a large mixing bowl. Add the grated onion, garlic, parsley, mint, dill, flour, lemon juice, eggs, remaining ¾ teaspoon of salt, and pepper. Flake the cooked fish into the bowl, taking care to remove any stray bones. Gently fold the mixture together until well combined. Scoop out about 1½ tablespoons of the mixture and form it into a small, uniform patty, 2½ to 3 inches in diameter, with impeccably clean hands. Continue in this fashion with the remaining fish mixture. You should end up with about 12 fish cakes.

Heat ¼ inch of the oil in a deep skillet or large sauté pan over medium heat until the oil shimmers (see tip, page 42). Working in batches, carefully add a few fish cakes at a time to the hot oil. Cook until golden, about 5 to 6 minutes per side. Add a little more oil to the pan as needed. Remove the finished fish cakes to an oven-safe platter lined with paper towels to drain. Keep the finished fish cakes warm in the oven until all have been fried. Serve immediately with the lemon wedges and the *Tzatziki*, *Mama's Domata Saltsa*, or tomato sauce, if desired.

Kalamarakia Tiganita (kah-lah-mah-RAH-kia tee-gha-nee-TAH)

LIGHTLY FRIED CALAMARI

Fried calamari (squid) is incredibly popular in Greece. However, squid is a tricky little creature in the kitchen. It should be cooked for only a minute or so, or cooked slowly for more than 30 minutes. Anything in between and you will feel like you're gnawing on an old tire. I call this recipe "lightly" fried because the fried calamari so famous in Greece is not like the typical, greasy, batter-drenched calamari found in many restaurants in America. Use a deep-fry thermometer to make sure your oil is at the correct temperature (350 degrees) to fry the squid quickly and completely without burning it.

SERVES 4 TO 6

Olive or vegetable oil for frying
2 cups all-purpose flour
1 tablespoon dried oregano
2½ teaspoons sea salt, plus more to taste
1½ teaspoons freshly ground black pepper
1 pound small (baby) squid with tentacles, cleaned (see tip), tubes cut into ½-inch rings, tentacles left whole
2 lemons, sliced into thick wedges
1 recipe *Tzatziki* (page 76) (optional)

Fill a large, deep saucepan or pot with oil 2 to 3 inches deep. Set over medium heat and, using a deep-fry thermometer, bring the oil to 350 degrees. Meanwhile, mix the flour, oregano, salt, and pepper in a shallow dish. Working in batches, dredge the squid in the flour mixture, coating it well. Use a metal sieve or colander to shake off any excess flour. Carefully add the squid to the hot oil and fry until crisp and lightly golden, about 1 minute for each batch. Do not overcook. Using tongs, a slotted metal spoon, or a fine-mesh strainer, lift the calamari out of the oil and onto a large dish lined with paper towels to drain.

Serve piping hot with a squeeze of lemon juice. To make this dish especially delicious, serve it with *Tzatziki*.

———————— 🇬🇷 ————————

YIAYIA'S TIP: Most of the squid you find at the market today has already been cleaned to some degree, but you may need to remove the transparent backbone (pen) from the body (mantle). Gently remove the blade-shape pen, along with any viscera, and the membrane that clings to it. To remove the tentacles, use kitchen shears to cut in front of the eyes, then remove the tentacles, discarding the beak and head. If you're buying whole, uncleaned squid for the first time, a quick Internet search will guide you to helpful tutorials.

Keftethes (kef-TEH-thes)

GREEK HAMBURGER PATTIES

Keftethes are typically served as an appetizer with *Tzatziki* (page 76). However, you can also serve these delicious morsels as a main course with *Pilafi* (page 230) or *Araka Lathera* (page 227). Traditionally, these hamburger patties are fried, but my baked version is light, healthy, and flavorful.

SERVES 4 TO 6

1 cup day-old bread, crusts removed, cut into
    ½-inch cubes (about 1 to 2 slices)

1½ pounds lean ground beef or turkey

1 medium yellow onion, finely chopped

3 tablespoons finely chopped fresh Italian
    flat-leaf parsley

½ teaspoon dried oregano

1 teaspoon finely chopped fresh mint

1 tablespoon freshly squeezed lemon juice (about
    ½ lemon)

1 tablespoon extra-virgin olive oil

2 large eggs

¾ teaspoon sea salt

½ teaspoon fresh ground black pepper

½ cup all-purpose flour

1 recipe *Tzatziki* (page 76) (optional)

Soak the bread briefly in a bowl of water until wet all the way the through. Squeeze the bread to remove excess water and transfer to a large mixing bowl. Add the ground beef or turkey, onion, parsley, oregano, mint, lemon juice, olive oil, eggs, salt, and pepper, and knead with impeccably clean hands until well combined. Cover the bowl and refrigerate for 1 hour.

Preheat oven to 350 degrees. Lightly oil a large baking dish.

Shape the meat mixture into individual patties, about 1-inch thick and 3 inches across. Spread the flour out on a large dish. Dredge each patty in the flour to lightly dust both sides and shake off any excess flour. Neatly arrange the patties in the prepared baking dish. Bake for 30 to 35 minutes. Serve immediately with *Tzatziki* on the side, if desired.

Kolokithakia Tiganita *(koh-loh-kee-THAH-kee-ah tee-gha-nee-TAH)*

LIGHTLY FRIED ZUCCHINI

Fried zucchini is a staple on nearly every menu in Greece. When it's prepared well, I am sure nothing on the planet tastes better. I don't trust anyone who does not like fried zucchini.

SERVES 4 TO 6

4 medium zucchini, sliced into ⅛- to ¼-inch rounds or matchsticks
1½ teaspoons sea salt, plus more as needed
½ teaspoon freshly ground pepper
1 cup all-purpose flour
½ cup olive or vegetable oil for frying, plus more as needed
1 lemon cut into large wedges
1 recipe *Tzatziki* (page 76) *or Skorthalia Made with Potatoes* (page 81) (optional)

Gently squeeze the zucchini slices over the sink to drain the excess water. Lightly season both sides of the zucchini slices with the salt and pepper. Spread the flour out on a large plate or baking dish. Dredge the zucchini in the flour and shake off any excess.

Heat the oil in a large sauté pan over medium heat until it shimmers, adding more if necessary to come ½ inch up the sides of the pan. Test the temperature of the oil by gently placing 1 zucchini slice into it. The oil should bubble pretty vigorously around the zucchini. Working in small batches, carefully slip the zucchini into the hot oil and cook briefly until crunchy and golden, about 4 to 5 minutes per side, watching carefully and turning to prevent burning.

Using a slotted metal spoon, transfer the fried zucchini to a large plate lined with paper towels to drain. Sprinkle again with a little more of the salt while piping hot, if desired. Serve immediately with the lemon wedges and with *Tzatziki* or *Skorthalia Made with Potatoes*, if desired. For a traditional treat, offer a shot of ouzo over ice.

Kolokithopites *(koh-loh-kee-THO-pee-tes)*

ZUCCHINI FRITTERS

This dish is traditionally made to use up the zucchini pulp that is left when making *Kolokithakia Gemista me Kima* (Stuffed Zucchini, page 202). Greek families feel it is disrespectful to waste food, so they always find a way to use every part of the fruit, the vegetables, or even the animals they are consuming. These fritters are charmingly rustic, so don't worry if they are not perfectly round.

SERVES 4 TO 6

3 pounds medium zucchini, washed and stemmed

1 teaspoon sea salt, divided

½ cup plus 1 tablespoon all-purpose flour

2 large eggs

¼ cup finely chopped fresh mint

½ teaspoon freshly ground black pepper

6 to 8 ounces brine-packed Greek feta (about 1½ cups), crumbled small

2 tablespoons finely grated kefalotiri or Parmesan cheese (optional)

Olive or vegetable oil for frying

1 recipe *Tzatziki* (page 76) (optional)

Preheat oven to 250 degrees.

Cut the zucchini in half down the center into half cylinders. With a small teaspoon or a grapefruit spoon, hollow out the zucchini skins by scooping out all the pulp, leaving about ⅛ inch of zucchini intact next to the skin. Leave the bottoms intact so that you are left with a "zucchini cup" that can be stuffed later. Take care not to crack or puncture the skins. Cover the zucchini skins and reserve in the refrigerator to make *Kolokithakia Gemista me Kima*.

Transfer the pulp to the bowl of a food processor or high-performance blender and pulse a few times to chop finely. Place the finely chopped zucchini pulp into a colander and toss with ½ teaspoon of the salt. Cover the zucchini with a plate and put a weight on top (such as a large can of tomatoes). Drain for 10 minutes, briefly rinse, then squeeze as much moisture as possible from the pulp with impeccably clean hands.

Whisk the flour, eggs, mint, remaining ½ teaspoon of salt, and pepper in a large mixing bowl until smooth. Gently fold the drained zucchini pulp into the flour mixture along with the feta and kefalotiri or Parmesan cheese (if using). Stir until the mixture resembles a thick batter.

In a deep skillet or Dutch oven set over medium heat, heat about ½ inch of the oil until it shimmers (see tip, page 42). Working in batches if necessary to prevent overcrowding, scoop out heaping tablespoons of the batter and carefully drop into the oil. The fritters will naturally flatten out. Cook for 3 to 5 minutes per side, until golden brown, flipping them over carefully, just as you would a pancake. Remove the fritters from the oil and drain on a large, oven-safe plate lined with paper towels. Keep fritters warm in the preheated oven as you continue to fry the remaining fritters in batches. Serve plain or with *Tzatziki.*

Melitzanosalata *(mel-tzah-NOH-sah-lah-TAH)*

EGGPLANT DIP

This is both my favorite way to eat eggplant and my very favorite Greek *mezze* dip. Even if you don't like eggplant, chances are you will like this recipe. It has an exquisite and unexpected flavor!

YIELDS 2½ CUPS

2½ to 3 pounds eggplant (2 to 3 medium eggplant)

½ cup chopped yellow onion

2 to 3 cloves garlic, to taste, chopped

2 to 3 tablespoons freshly squeezed lemon juice (1 lemon)

1 teaspoon sea salt, plus more to taste

¼ teaspoon freshly ground black pepper

6 Kalamata olives, pitted

¼ cup extra-virgin olive oil, plus more as needed

3 tablespoons finely chopped fresh Italian flat-leaf parsley

¼ cup brine-packed Greek feta, crumbled small (optional)

Preheat oven to 425 degrees. Line a sheet pan with aluminum foil or unbleached parchment paper.

Prick the eggplant with a fork in a few places all around to allow steam to escape while cooking. Put the eggplant on the lined sheet pan and bake for 40 to 45 minutes or until very tender. Remove from oven and place the hot eggplant on a large plate lined with paper towels to cool and drain.

When cool enough to handle, remove the stems and slice each eggplant in half. Peel the eggplant and use a spoon to scrape any remaining pulp from the skins. Discard the skins and scrape away as many seeds as possible from the pulp. Transfer the pulp to the bowl of a food processor or high-performance blender. Add the onion, garlic, lemon juice, salt, pepper, and olives. Blend together until just combined. Then, with the motor running, slowly drizzle the olive oil into the mixture, blending until it resembles cream of wheat or hummus. Eggplant tend to have a naturally creamy consistency, so you may not need to add all the olive oil. Alternatively, if you wish to have a looser consistency, you may add more oil, 1 tablespoon at a time, to reach the desired consistency.

Transfer the eggplant mixture to a large bowl and fold in the parsley. Cover and refrigerate for 2 hours or up to a full day, so that the flavors can come together. Just before serving, sprinkle the crumbled feta cheese (if using) on top as a garnish. Serve with oven-warmed or grilled pita bread or a selection of fresh vegetables for dipping.

DEBBIE'S TIP: Omit the feta cheese for a vegan *Melitzanosalata.*

Taramosalata *(tah-rah-MOH-sah-lah-TAH)*

FISH ROE DIP

This is Greek caviar! *Taramosalata* is traditionally made with the salted and cured pink roe from carp, which gives this salty dip its signature pink color. Over the years, other blends of fish roe have become common as well, depending on what is locally available. Like any caviar, it's an acquired taste. Enjoy it slathered on a warm piece of bread or pita with a small glass of ice-cold ouzo.

YIELDS 2 CUPS

5 to 6 thick slices day-old bread, crusts removed

4 tablespoons tarama (carp roe, or other pink caviar)

2 tablespoons finely chopped yellow onion

¾ cup extra-virgin olive oil

4 tablespoons freshly squeezed lemon juice (about 2 lemons)

Soak the bread briefly in a bowl of water until wet all the way the through. Squeeze the bread to remove excess water, tear it into small pieces, and set aside.

Blend the tarama and onion in a food processor or high-performance blender for about 1 minute until smooth and well mixed. Add the bread to the tarama mixture and blend again until just combined. Then, with the motor running, slowly drizzle in the olive oil until the mixture resembles a thick paste. Keep the motor running and add the lemon juice slowly, 1 tablespoon at a time. Blend until smooth and creamy.

Serve immediately or refrigerate for up to 2 days.

Fasolia Pouree *(fah-SOH-lee-ah POO-reh)*

WHITE BEAN PURÉE

This recipe is very similar to a traditional hummus, but as it's made with white beans, it has a lighter, creamier texture. You'll find some version of a white bean purée on nearly every Greek restaurant table. Usually it is accompanied by *melitzanosalata* and *taramosalata*. It's delicious as a dip, on sandwiches, or spread on crackers with olives on top. It keeps for up to 1 week in the refrigerator. Because it is great the day after you make it, it's a perfect make-ahead item for a big party.

YIELDS ABOUT 2¼ CUPS

FOR THE BEANS

1 cup (½ pound) small dried white beans (I like cannellini), soaked for 8 hours or overnight

2 cloves garlic, smashed

2 bay leaves

¾ teaspoon sea salt

FOR THE PURÉE

¼ cup freshly squeezed lemon juice (about 2 lemons)

¼ to ½ cup extra-virgin olive oil, to taste

2 garlic cloves, roughly chopped

1½ teaspoons ground cumin

¼ teaspoon sea salt, plus more to taste

Freshly ground black pepper, to taste

Drain and rinse the soaked beans. Transfer the beans to a large stockpot and cover with fresh water by 1 inch. Bring to a boil over medium-high heat and cook for 3 minutes, skimming off any foam or scum that rises to the surface. Reduce heat to low, add the garlic and bay leaves, and simmer, covered with a tilted lid, for 30 minutes. Stir in the salt, replace the tilted lid, and continue cooking for another 20 to 30 minutes or until the beans are very tender. Remove from heat and let the beans cool to room temperature, uncovered, in their cooking liquid.

When the beans have cooled, discard the bay leaves and the smashed garlic and drain well. Place the beans in a food processor or high-performance blender. Add the lemon juice, ¼ cup of olive oil, chopped garlic, cumin, salt, and a few grinds of black pepper. Process until smooth and thick.

Taste and adjust seasonings if necessary. Add a little more olive oil to taste, if desired. Transfer to a small bowl, cover, and refrigerate for 2 hours or until well chilled. Serve cold with Kalamata olives, crudités, and/or warm pita triangles. You can also use as a spread for sandwiches. I like to dust the top with a little smoked paprika right before serving.

DEBBIE'S TIP: No time to make beans from scratch? No problem! You can easily make this recipe with canned beans. Use 2 (15-ounce) cans small white beans, like cannellini or great northern. Be sure to drain and rinse the beans very well, and then proceed with the recipe.

Gavros *(GAH-vrose)*

GREEK FLASH-FRIED FISH

Gavros are fresh, uncured European anchovies. They are abundant in the Mediterranean region, especially in Greece, Italy, Spain, the south of France, Bulgaria, Turkey, and Croatia. You probably will not find them in an American market, but if you do happen to come across them, consider yourself very lucky! They are absolutely delicious when flash fried. In America, Greek cooks often substitute smelts for *gavros,* as they are quite similar.

SERVES 4 TO 6

1 pound whole smelts, heads and fins removed, gutted
1½ cups all-purpose flour
Olive or vegetable oil for frying
1 teaspoon salt
2 lemons, cut into wedges for serving

Wash the fish under cold water, and pat dry with paper towels. Spread the flour on a large plate or baking dish.

Heat 1 inch of oil in a large sauté pan over medium-high heat until the oil shimmers. Season the fish with the salt, dredge it in the flour, and shake off any excess. Fry the fish in the oil, working in batches to prevent overcrowding, until golden brown and cooked through, about 3 to 4 minutes per side. Transfer the cooked fish to a large dish lined with paper towels to drain. Squeeze a couple of lemon wedges over the top of the fish, and serve immediately with the remaining lemon wedges.

YIAYIA'S TIP: You can also use small fresh sardines if smelts are unavailable. Ask your fishmonger to prepare the fish for you if you're squeamish about gutting them. Don't worry about boning them, as the bones are edible.

Octopothi sta Karvouna *(octo-POH-thee stah KAR-voo-nah)*

GRILLED OCTOPUS

Grilled octopus has a delicious flavor. This recipe came from a local *taverna* in Fanari, a lovely village in northern Greece on the Aegean Sea where my parents have had a home for years. The owner of the *taverna* was kind enough to share his secret with me—he boils the octopus in water flavored with Coca-Cola to tenderize it! This surprising trick yields excellent results.

SERVES 4

12 cups water

½ cup plus 2 tablespoons extra-virgin olive oil, divided

1 (12-ounce) can Coca-Cola Classic

2 bay leaves

2 (1½-pound) octopuses, cleaned and gutted, with eyes, beak, and ink sac removed (see tip)

2 tablespoons red wine vinegar

1½ teaspoons dried oregano, plus more to taste

½ teaspoon freshly ground teaspoon pepper

Sea salt (optional, to taste)

2 medium tomatoes, cut into ¼-inch slices

Bring the water to a boil in a large pot set over high heat. Add 2 tablespoons of the olive oil, the Coca-Cola, and the bay leaves, and stir to combine. Carefully submerge the octopuses in the liquid and return to a boil. Cook, uncovered, over medium-high heat for 45 minutes. Drain the octopuses and let them cool.

While the octopuses are cooling, prepare a charcoal grill with a very hot fire or set a gas grill to high. When the octopuses are cool enough to handle, run them under cold water, and rub off as much of the dark outer skin as you can. (It is fine to leave a little behind.) Use a large, very sharp kitchen knife to cut the tentacles from the center sections, keeping the tentacles whole. Reserve the center sections for another use.

Using a large pastry brush, brush the grill with ¼ cup of the olive oil to prevent sticking. Lay the tentacles on the oiled grill and cook for 4 to 5 minutes on each side, until tender and slightly charred. Remove from the grill and toss with the remaining ¼ cup of olive oil, vinegar, oregano, pepper, and salt (if using). Lay the tomato slices on a large serving dish or divide them among individual plates, top with the octopus tentacles, and serve.

DEBBIE'S TIP: Octopus can be very salty on its own. Taste it *after* you have tossed it with all the other required ingredients. If you think it needs a little salt, add a pinch to taste. You may find it doesn't need any additional salt.

YIAYIA'S TIP: If you buy your octopus from a reputable fishmonger, it's likely that it's already been cleaned and tenderized for you. In the fishing villages of Greece, the fishermen gently beat fresh octopuses from the sea against the rocks to tenderize them before they take them to the market to sell. If you are fortunate enough to catch your own octopus, beat it with a meat cleaver or mallet 40 to 50 times and rinse away the foam before you boil it, so that it does not turn out rubbery!

Saltses
BASIC SAUCES

Greeks do not typically use condiments like mustard, mayonnaise, ketchup, and steak sauce that are found on the American table. Most salads in Greece are dressed with a simple lemon or vinegar and extra-virgin olive oil dressing. There are not hundreds of varieties of salad dressings to choose from. In fact, there is actually no word in the Greek language for "salad dressing." Instead, Greeks tend to favor relatively simple dressings and sauces cooked fresh and made with only a few select ingredients. Key flavors in most Greek sauces include lemon, garlic, parsley, and dill. When you begin to embrace cooking this way, you will be amazed at how vibrant the flavors of your favorite foods will become. The sauces in this chapter are used in recipes throughout this book.

Avgolemono *(ah-VGHO-leh-moh-noh)*

EGG-LEMON SAUCE

In Greek, the word *avgolemono* means "egg lemon." This sauce is one of the most versatile and widely used sauces in all of Greek cooking, and it is a great addition to anyone's repertoire. Use it to dress up your favorite dish, add it to soup to thicken and add delicious flavor, or pour it over *Dolmathes me Lahano* (Stuffed Cabbage, page 199), *Youvarlakia* (Greek Meatball Soup, page 146), or *Kolokithakia Gemista me Kima* (Stuffed Zucchini, page 202). As you will see with the recipes in this book, this sauce often is made from the cooking liquid or broth of whatever dish you are preparing.

YIELDS 2 CUPS

2 large eggs

¼ cup plus 2 tablespoons freshly squeezed lemon juice (2 to 3 lemons)

1 cup hot (not boiling) chicken or vegetable broth (or fish broth if using with a fish soup)

In a medium mixing bowl, beat the eggs with a whisk until they are frothy. Gradually whisk in the lemon juice until combined. Slowly add the hot broth, a little at a time, being careful not to add it too quickly (see tip).

If using this recipe in soup, slowly add the mixture to the soup, stirring constantly. If using as a sauce, transfer to a saucepan, set over very low heat, and simmer, stirring constantly, until slightly thickened.

———————— 🇬🇷 ————————

YIAYIA'S TIP: Slowly incorporating the hot broth into the egg mixture while whisking vigorously is a technique called tempering. For best results, have your eggs at room temperature and the broth hot but not boiling. Adding the broth too quickly will result in a wet mess of scrambled eggs. Don't be intimidated! Do it once, and you will forever have a knack for tempering.

Béchamel Sauce *(BEH-shah-mel)*

This is the recipe for my mom's very decadent *Béchamel Sauce,* which is a fun calorie splurge that I enjoy occasionally. If you want a lighter, lower-calorie sauce, omit the feta and use reduced-fat milk.

YIELDS 4 CUPS

½ cup (1 stick) unsalted butter
½ cup flour
4 cups hot (not boiling) milk
2 egg yolks, beaten
½ teaspoon sea salt
¼ teaspoon freshly ground black pepper
¼ cup grated kefalotiri or Parmesan cheese
¼ cup brine-packed Greek feta cheese (optional)

Melt the butter slowly in a medium saucepan over medium-low heat, being careful not burn or brown it. Slowly add the flour, stirring with a wooden spoon and mixing until smooth. Continue to cook for 2 minutes, stirring constantly, until the flour is golden and smells toasty. Do not brown.

Remove from heat and very slowly pour in the hot milk, stirring constantly. Set the sauce back over medium heat and simmer while stirring constantly until the sauce is smooth and thick, about 7 to 10 minutes.

Remove from heat. Temper the egg yolks in a large, heatproof mixing bowl by slowly adding about 1 cup of the hot milk mixture to them, stirring quickly. Then slowly stir the tempered egg yolks back into the hot milk mixture. If the béchamel seems too thick at this point, do not panic. Continue to stir and stir and eventually it will lighten up and become smooth again. Add the salt, pepper, kefalotiri or Parmesan cheese, and feta (if using), stirring to combine well. Use immediately.

Latholemono

(lah-thoh-LEH-moh-noh)

LEMON–OLIVE OIL DRESSING

This classic and very versatile dressing is one of my all-time favorites. Sometimes the simplest things really are the best. Try this dressing on salads, fish, shellfish—even chicken. I *love* it on *Horta* (Dandelion Greens Salad, page 104).

SERVES 6 TO 8

4 to 6 tablespoons freshly squeezed lemon juice (2 to 3 lemons), depending on how tangy you like it

½ teaspoon sea salt, or to taste

¼ teaspoon freshly ground black pepper, or to taste

1 clove garlic, minced (optional)

½ cup extra-virgin olive oil

In a small bowl, whisk the lemon juice, salt, pepper, and garlic (if using). Then very slowly drizzle in the olive oil, whisking constantly to emulsify. Serve immediately or refrigerate until ready to use.

Mama's Domata Saltsa *(mah-MAH's doh-MAH-tah SAL-tsah)*

MOM'S STEWED TOMATOES

This is a simple way to make a garden-fresh tomato sauce, which adds a great tomato base to many Greek dishes, such as *Gigantes* (page 183). Using fresh tomatoes rather than canned makes a big difference in flavor. I love it!

YIELDS 4 CUPS

2½ pounds (about 3 to 4 large) tomatoes, whole, with stems and cores removed

3 cups water

2 tablespoons tomato paste

½ teaspoon sea salt, plus more to taste

¼ teaspoon freshly ground black pepper, plus more to taste

Place the tomatoes and water in a medium saucepan and bring to a boil over medium-high heat. Boil for 1 minute, then remove the tomatoes with a slotted spoon and submerge them in a large bowl of ice water. Quickly slip their skins off and return them to the cooking water. Set over medium-high heat and return to a boil. Reduce heat to medium-low, cover, and cook for 30 minutes, until the tomatoes are tender.

Remove the saucepan from the heat and mash the tomatoes into a chunky purée with a large fork or potato masher. To prevent lumps of tomato paste, ladle a cup of the tomato mash into a small bowl and add the tomato paste, stirring to combine completely. Stir the tomato paste mixture back into the tomatoes in the saucepan and add the salt and pepper. Cook, uncovered and stirring frequently, over medium heat, until the mixture has reduced to a thick chunky sauce, about 20 minutes more. Remove from heat, taste, and season with additional salt and pepper, if necessary.

DEBBIE'S TIP: Take advantage of ripe, juicy tomatoes in season by doubling or even tripling this recipe. Stewed tomatoes will keep in the freezer for up to a year, so you can enjoy fresh tomato flavor all winter long.

Yiaourti Lemoni kai Anitho (yah-OOR-tee leh-MOH-nee keh AH-nee-thoh)

YOGURT LEMON DILL SAUCE

This is a really easy, versatile sauce. Cooling and refreshing, it whips up in a flash and can dress up a simple meal. Add some capers for texture and some extra flavor. Serve it as a sauce for fish, fried calamari, fried zucchini, or chicken or as a dip for raw vegetables.

YIELDS 2 CUPS

2 cups plain Greek yogurt

2 teaspoons grated lemon zest (1 lemon)

2 to 3 tablespoons freshly squeezed lemon juice (1 lemon)

¼ cup finely minced fresh dill

1 tablespoon capers, rinsed and drained well, roughly chopped (optional)

⅛ teaspoon sea salt

¼ teaspoon freshly ground black pepper

Stir all ingredients together in a small bowl. Cover and refrigerate until ready to use. Serve cold.

———————— ≣ ————————

DEBBIE'S TIP: I like to make this sauce a couple of hours ahead of time and let it stand in the refrigerator so that the flavors have a chance to marry. You can truly make this sauce your way. If you like more or less of any of the ingredients, adjust to your taste and enjoy. You can make this sauce up to 1 day ahead of time.

Tzatziki *(dza-DZEE-kee)*

GARLIC YOGURT CUCUMBER SAUCE

Tzatziki is one of the best-known Greek culinary exports. Although you could potentially kill a vampire after eating it, I strongly believe that the more garlicky kick it has, the better it tastes. Still, I would not recommend partaking of this spicy spread before a business meeting or a hot date. When I was a teen spending my summers in Greece, my cousins and I would never eat *tzatziki* before going out to the clubs . . . especially if we were trying to impress the boys!

Like ketchup on an American hamburger, *tzatziki* is ubiquitous on a *gyro*. Try it as a sauce for fish, or enjoy it as an appetizer or a snack with chunks of country bread. Whichever way you choose to enjoy it, if you like garlic, you'll love this recipe.

YIELDS 2½ CUPS

½ seedless English cucumber, peeled
1 teaspoon sea salt, divided, plus more to taste
2 cups plain Greek yogurt
3 cloves garlic, peeled and mashed into a paste
⅓ cup extra-virgin olive oil
1 tablespoon red or white wine vinegar
1 tablespoon minced fresh dill

Coarsely grate the cucumber using a box grater or food processor and toss with ½ teaspoon of the salt. Place the grated cucumber in a fine-mesh sieve set over a bowl and drain for 10 minutes. Working in batches, a handful at a time, squeeze as much remaining water from the cucumber as possible, transferring the drained cucumber to a medium mixing bowl.

Add the rest of the ingredients along with the remaining ½ teaspoon of salt, and mix well. You can serve the *Tzatziki* immediately, but I prefer to let it sit in refrigerator for 2 to 3 hours so that all of the flavors blend and come alive. *Tzatziki* will keep for up to 5 days in the refrigerator, but be warned: the garlicky flavor intensifies as time passes!

Early morning coffee at the local *cafenio* with the men of the village of Fanari.

Skorthalia (skor-thah-LEEYA)

GARLIC SAUCE MADE WITH POTATOES

Skorthalia has a real kick. The literal translation of the Greek word *skorthalia* is "garlic dip," and trust me, it really delivers. If *tzatziki* can kill one vampire, this recipe can wipe out the whole vampire village. It is often served as an accompaniment to cod. I will never forget the first time my brother-in-law came over to a family gathering. He mistook the bowl of *skorthalia* sitting beside the cod for mashed potatoes and piled a few heaping spoonfuls onto his plate. After shoveling a very healthy bite into his mouth and swallowing, his face turned six shades of red, and he quickly realized just how potent this condiment can be. Twenty-five years later, we are still laughing about that day.

YIELDS 1½ CUPS

4 large Yukon Gold potatoes, peeled
2 tablespoons plus 1½ teaspoons sea salt, plus
   more to taste
5 cloves garlic
¾ cup extra-virgin olive oil
2 tablespoons freshly squeezed lemon juice
   (1 lemon)

Cut the peeled potatoes into 2-inch chunks and place them in a large pot. Add enough cold water to cover the potatoes and stir in 2 tablespoons of the salt. Bring to a boil over medium-high heat, reduce heat to medium, and cook for 15 to 20 minutes, until tender. Drain in a colander and immediately transfer the hot potatoes to a high-performance blender or food processor. Add the garlic and the remaining 1½ teaspoons of salt and process until smooth and well combined. With the motor running, slowly drizzle in the olive oil, followed by the lemon juice. Taste and add more salt, if necessary.

Serve at room temperature. *Skorthalia* will last up to 5 days, covered, in the refrigerator.

—MADE WITH WALNUTS

YIELDS 1½ CUPS

1 cup walnut halves
4 cloves garlic
1½ teaspoons sea salt, plus more to taste
¾ cup extra-virgin olive oil
½ cup white wine vinegar

Combine the walnuts, garlic, and salt in a high-performance blender or food processor. Pulse until the mixture resembles a fine meal. With the motor running, slowly drizzle in the olive oil, followed by the vinegar. Taste and add additional salt, if necessary.

Serve at room temperature. *Skorthalia* will last up to 5 days, covered, in the refrigerator.

Tahini Sauce

I love to throw big parties with lots of food and fun. Since many of my friends are vegan, I came up with this sauce to serve as an alternative to yogurt-based sauces. Try it as a dip for raw veggies, paired with cucumbers and sliced red onion, as a salad dressing, or as a sauce for fish or chicken.

YIELDS ABOUT 1½ CUPS

½ cup tahini (sesame seed paste)

¼ cup freshly squeezed lemon juice (about 2 lemons)

2 tablespoons extra-virgin olive oil

1 clove garlic, minced

1 tablespoon finely chopped fresh Italian flat-leaf parsley

1 teaspoon finely chopped fresh mint (optional)

½ teaspoon sea salt, plus more to taste

¼ teaspoon freshly ground black pepper

¼ cup water, plus more as needed

Whisk together the tahini and the lemon juice. Slowly drizzle in the olive oil, whisking constantly, to form a smooth emulsion. Add the garlic, parsley, mint (if using), salt, and pepper, and stir to combine. Slowly add the water, 1 teaspoon at a time, to achieve desired consistency.

Taste and adjust seasonings, if necessary. Serve immediately or refrigerate, covered, for up to 3 days.

DEBBIE'S TIP: Parsley is a universally used herb that brightens up just about any savory dish. But if you are not a fan or you want to mix it up, you can substitute dill, or use a combination of dill and parsley.

Summer Peach Salsa

When peaches are in season, I eat them nearly every day. Summer peaches in Greece are huge and incredibly fragrant, so I created this salsa in their honor. It pairs well with simply grilled fish and chicken.

Although it's not traditionally Greek, I make this salsa often because we have an abundance of fresh peaches from the peach trees in our yard.

YIELDS 3½ CUPS

2 large ripe peaches, diced medium (about 2 cups)

2 ripe medium tomatoes, diced medium (about 1 cup)

½ large red onion, diced small (about 1 cup)

3 tablespoons finely chopped fresh Italian flat-leaf parsley

1 jalapeño pepper, seeds and white pith removed, finely chopped (optional)

2 tablespoons freshly squeezed lemon juice (1 lemon)

2 tablespoons extra-virgin olive oil

¼ teaspoon sea salt, plus more to taste

¼ teaspoon freshly ground black pepper

In a medium mixing bowl, gently stir together all the ingredients.

Taste and adjust seasonings, if necessary. You can make this salsa a few hours ahead, cover, and refrigerate to allow all the flavors to come together.

VARIATION: For an interesting flavor and a little more crunch, use 1 cup peeled, diced cucumber in place of the tomatoes.

———— 🇬🇷 ————

DEBBIE'S TIP: Like your salsa spicier? Don't remove the seeds and white pith of the jalapeño pepper. That will add some more heat.

Salates
SALADS

Salads in Greece are served seasonally, meaning typically they are comprised of whatever local fresh vegetables happen to be available at the market that day. For example, when we were in Greece shooting photos for this book, we searched high and low for cabbage. The response we met with was simply, "I'm sorry, the farmer didn't bring it today." Greeks find cabbage unpalatable until after the first frost, and farmers won't even consider bringing substandard vegetables to market. One of the primary reasons the Mediterranean diet is so healthy is that as much as 80 percent of it is composed of fresh seasonal fruits and vegetables. When you sit down to a meal in Greece, most of the space on your plate is devoted to vegetables and salads. The salads in this chapter are light, simple, delicious, and healthy. Like most traditional Greek food, they are served family style. As you can see in the opposite picture of my Aunt Aphrodite (on the right) and my mom (in the background), making Greek salads is a family affair!

Horiatki Salata *(hor-YIA-tee-kee sah-lah-TAH)*

GREEK VILLAGE SALAD

Unlike many of the Greek salads found on menus in America, traditional Greek village salads do not contain lettuce. This salad is a staple of nearly every Greek lunch and dinner. Serve it with any of the main dishes in this book for a wholesome, rustic, and traditional supper you and your family will adore.

SERVES 4 TO 6

1 seedless English cucumber, peeled and sliced

4 to 5 large ripe tomatoes, sliced into wedges

1 large red onion, sliced

1 large green bell pepper, sliced

1 cup Kalamata olives, plus more to taste

¼ pound brine-packed Greek feta cheese, drained and sliced lengthwise

1 teaspoon dried oregano

2 tablespoons capers, rinsed and drained (optional)

2 to 3 tablespoons freshly squeezed lemon juice (1 lemon)

⅓ cup extra-virgin olive oil

1 lemon cut into wedges, to serve with salad

Sea salt (optional)

Toss the cucumber, tomatoes, onion, bell pepper, and olives together in a large salad bowl and top with the slices of feta. Crush the oregano in your hand to release its fragrant essential oils, then sprinkle over the salad along with capers (if using). Drizzle the lemon juice over the salad, then the olive oil. Set aside to marinate at room temperature for 20 minutes, or serve immediately with some lemon wedges alongside for added zest. The feta is quite salty, which usually eliminates the need for added salt. Give the salad a taste just before serving, and sprinkle a pinch of salt over the tomatoes and cucumbers, if desired.

Pligouri Salata *(plee-GHOO-ree sah-lah-TAH)*

BULGUR WHEAT SALAD

Bulgur wheat is a grain used often in Greece. This nutty, quick-cooking salad is a surprisingly refreshing crowd pleaser.

SERVES 6 TO 8

4 tablespoons extra-virgin olive oil, divided

1 medium yellow onion, diced small

1 cup bulgur wheat

1 cup low-sodium vegetable broth or water

3 medium tomatoes, cored and diced

3 scallions, white and soft green parts, thinly sliced

1 clove garlic, finely chopped

¼ cup finely chopped fresh Italian flat-leaf parsley

1 tablespoon finely chopped fresh mint

¼ cup chopped walnuts

1 tablespoon lemon zest (1 lemon)

2 to 3 tablespoons freshly squeezed lemon juice (1 lemon)

½ teaspoon sea salt

¼ teaspoon freshly ground black pepper

Heat 2 tablespoons of the olive oil in a medium saucepan set over medium heat. Add the onion and sauté until translucent, about 5 to 6 minutes, stirring frequently. Add the bulgur wheat and stir to coat with olive oil–onion mixture. Add the vegetable broth or water, increase heat to medium-high, and bring to a boil. Reduce heat to medium-low and simmer, uncovered, for 4 minutes. Remove from heat, cover, and set aside for 10 minutes.

Meanwhile, combine the tomatoes, scallions, garlic, parsley, mint, walnuts, and lemon zest in a large mixing or serving bowl. Toss to combine.

Fluff the bulgur wheat with a fork and add it to the bowl. Add the lemon juice, the remaining 2 tablespoons of olive oil, salt, and pepper, and mix gently to combine. Let stand for 10 minutes for the flavors to come together, and serve. Alternatively, cover and refrigerate for up to 2 hours before serving.

Fakes Salata *(fah-KESS sah-lah-TAH)*

COLD LENTIL SALAD

Lentils are incredibly versatile and delicious. They are earthy, packed with iron and protein, and can be served hot or cold. I love this salad because it is unusual and refreshing, and it can even be served as a main course on a hot summer night.

SERVES 4

1 cup brown or French lentils, picked over, rinsed very well, and drained

2 cloves garlic, smashed and peeled

2 bay leaves

2 sprigs fresh thyme

3 cups water

¼ cup diced red onion

¼ cup finely chopped fresh Italian flat-leaf parsley

2 teaspoons lemon zest (1 lemon)

2 to 3 tablespoons freshly squeezed lemon juice (1 lemon)

2 tablespoons extra-virgin olive oil, divided

½ teaspoon sea salt

¼ teaspoon freshly ground black pepper

4 cups loosely packed mixed greens

2 ripe medium tomatoes, cut into wedges

1 recipe *Latholemono* (page 73)

Stir together the lentils, garlic, bay leaves, thyme, and water in a large pot set over medium-high heat, and bring to a boil. Boil for 2 minutes, reduce heat to medium-low, and simmer, covered with a tilted lid, for 30 to 40 minutes or until the lentils are tender. Remove from heat and discard the garlic, bay leaves, and thyme. Drain the lentils well in a sieve and let them cool to room temperature.

Transfer the lentils to a medium mixing bowl. Add the red onion, parsley, lemon zest, lemon juice, olive oil, salt, and pepper. Stir to combine. Set aside.

Toss the greens and tomatoes together with the *Latholemono* to taste.

Divide the greens and tomatoes evenly among four dinner plates, forming a bed for the lentils. Spoon an equal portion of lentils onto each bed of greens and tomatoes. Serve immediately.

———————— ▰ ————————

DEBBIE'S TIP: A number of varieties of lentils are available in the market today. I sometimes make this salad with black Beluga lentils or red lentils just to mix it up. If you do try a different variety of lentils, double check the cooking time on the package. Some cook longer, some shorter.

Dakos *(DAH-kohs)*

GREEK BRUSCHETTA

This is a traditional *mezze* salad from the island of Crete. I just love it. In Greece, this salad is served atop a barley rusk, called a *paximadi*. A rusk is just a form of hard bread that has been twice-baked to achieve crispness. You usually can find barley rusks in Mediterranean specialty shops or other gourmet markets. Choose very ripe, almost overly so, tomatoes so that their juice will really soak into the rusk beneath them. To make this vegan, just add another tomato and omit the feta.

SERVES 4 TO 6

1 large barley rusk, about 7 inches or so in
    diameter

Extra-virgin olive oil, to taste

2 large or 3 medium tomatoes, cored and diced

½ teaspoon sea salt, plus more to taste

½ teaspoon freshly ground black pepper

1 pound brine-packed Greek feta, crumbled small

2 tablespoons chopped fresh dill

2 teaspoons dried oregano

Lightly brush the flat top of the rusk with some of the olive oil. Mound the diced tomatoes on top and season them with nearly all of the salt and pepper, reserving about ⅛ teaspoon of each. Layer the feta on top of the tomatoes and evenly sprinkle the dill, oregano, and remaining salt and pepper on top of the cheese. Finally, drizzle olive oil to taste over the top and serve family style.

DEBBIE'S TIP: Can't find a barley rusk? No problem! Simply buy a large round loaf of crusty, bakery-fresh bread and slice it in half horizontally. If serving on a plate instead of in a bowl, cut a thin slice off the top half so that it will sit flat on the plate without tipping over. Brush the cut side of the top half with olive oil. Set the bottom half aside for another use. Toast on a baking sheet in a 400-degree oven until very crispy and golden, about 10 minutes. Watch carefully to make sure it doesn't burn. To make the bread extra crispy, turn on the broiler for 1 or 2 minutes and crack the oven door slightly. Again, watch carefully because your bread can go from golden to charcoal in 10 seconds flat.

Lahanosalata *(la-ha-NOH-sah-lah-TAH)*

CABBAGE AND CARROT SALAD

I *love, love, love* this salad! It is so light and simple yet so flavorful and filling. I seriously could eat the whole family-size recipe myself. Something about the clean flavors in this sensational cabbage salad creates the perfect sensory experience for your taste buds.

SERVES 4 TO 6

1 large head green or red cabbage, cored and shredded

2 cups coarsely shredded carrots

1 recipe *Latholemono* (page 73)

¼ teaspoon sea salt, plus more to taste

¼ teaspoon freshly ground black pepper

In a large mixing bowl, toss together the cabbage and carrots. Spoon on the *Latholemono,* a little bit at a time, until the salad is dressed lightly to your taste. Season with salt and pepper and serve immediately.

To make a few hours ahead, toss together the carrots and cabbage and keep the mixture in the refrigerator. Just before serving, add the *Latholemono* and season with salt and pepper.

Tomato, Cucumber, and Red Onion Salad

This fantastic summer salad is so easy to prepare. It pairs well with lamb, fish, chicken, and vegetarian main dishes alike.

SERVES 4

1 seedless English cucumber, unpeeled, sliced into
   1-inch chunks
4 to 5 large ripe tomatoes, sliced into wedges
1 large red onion, thinly sliced into half-moons
1 to 2 tablespoons finely chopped fresh Italian
   flat-leaf parsley or fresh dill
1 recipe *Latholemono* (page 73)
Sea salt, to taste
Freshly ground black pepper, to taste

Toss the cucumber, tomatoes, onion, and parsley or dill together in a large salad bowl. Add the *Latholemono*. Season with salt and pepper to taste and set aside to marinate at room temperature for up to 1 hour.

VARIATION: For a more soothing and cooling salad, leave out the red onion. For a crunchier salad, leave out the tomato. If you'd like a more acidic salad to pair with a rich main course, omit the cucumber. In other words, make it your own!

Patata kai Kremithi Salata *(pah-TAH-tah keh kreh-MEE-thee sah-lah-TAH)*

POTATO AND ONION SALAD

This easy potato and onion salad is my all-time favorite Greek salad next to the classic *Horiatki Salata* (page 86). Steaming the potatoes yields a tastier, firmer, and more nutritious result than boiling, as it keeps the potatoes from getting waterlogged and helps them absorb the dressing.

SERVES 6 TO 8

5 large russet potatoes, peeled and cut into
    1-inch chunks
1 large red onion, thinly sliced
¾ teaspoon sea salt, plus more to taste
½ teaspoon freshly ground black pepper
3 tablespoons extra-virgin olive oil
2 tablespoons red wine vinegar
3 tablespoons chopped fresh Italian
    flat-leaf parsley
½ cup capers, rinsed and drained

In a medium saucepan with a tight-fitting lid, steam the potatoes in a vegetable steamer over 2 inches of water for 20 to 25 minutes, until tender. Transfer the cooked potatoes to a large serving dish. Add the onion and season with the salt and pepper.

Whisk together the olive oil, vinegar, parsley, and capers in a small mixing bowl. Pour the oil mixture over the potatoes and onions. Serve warm.

Patzaria (pah-DZAR-ee-ah)

BEET SALAD

This was one of my favorite salads growing up and it still is. Healthy, simple, easy to prepare, and delicious, it is outstanding hot for dinner or cold for lunch the next day. I prefer mine really tangy, so I add extra vinegar. Have it the way you like it!

SERVES 4 TO 6

1½ pounds fresh medium red beets with
    greens attached
2 cloves garlic, finely chopped
½ teaspoon sea salt, plus more to taste
1 tablespoon white or red wine vinegar, plus
    more as needed
2 tablespoons extra-virgin olive oil, plus more
    as needed

Wash, scrub, and trim the beets. Pluck the greens off the tops. Wash and dry the greens and set them aside.

In a large pot set over high heat, boil the beets in plenty of salted water for 35 to 45 minutes, depending on their size, until tender. Drain the beets and when cool enough to handle, slip the skins off. You may want to wear disposable plastic or latex kitchen gloves when peeling the beets to prevent the beet juice from dyeing your hands red.

When the beets are nearly done cooking, boil the beet greens in another large pot of salted water for 5 to 15 minutes, until tender. Younger beet greens cook faster than more mature ones, so after 5 minutes of cooking, test them every few minutes for doneness. Using tongs, a slotted spoon, or a small strainer, carefully remove the beet greens from the water, drain in a colander, and arrange them at the center of a large serving platter.

Cut the beets into ¼-inch slices and arrange them in a circular or decorative pattern around the beet greens in the center of the serving dish. Sprinkle the chopped garlic evenly over the beets only. Sprinkle the salt over the beets and the greens, and then dress everything with the vinegar followed by the oil. Taste and adjust seasoning and/or dressing, if needed. Serve immediately.

Stopped by Sun & Sea, our favorite *taverna* in the village of Fanari, to visit with Kosmas Doukakis and his daughter and get his secret Grilled Octopus recipe (page 66).

Horta (HOR-tah)

DANDELION GREENS SALAD

Greeks have been doing juice cleanses since the dawn of time. The cooking liquid from this recipe is a fantastic, cleansing juice. Once the dandelion greens are done, reserve the liquid, chill it in the refrigerator, and enjoy.

SERVES 4

1 scant tablespoon sea salt, plus more to taste
1 large bunch dandelion greens
1 recipe *Latholemono* (page 73)
¼ cup Kalamata olives, for garnish
1 lemon, sliced, for garnish (optional)

Set a large pot of water over high heat and bring to a boil. Add 1 scant tablespoon of sea salt to the water.

Wash the dandelion greens in several changes of cold water and shake to remove excess water. Cut the greens into thirds and boil for 25 to 30 minutes or until very tender. With tongs, a slotted spoon, or a small strainer, carefully remove the greens from the water, allowing excess water to run back into the pot. Remove the water from the heat, let cool, and transfer to a pitcher or a bowl. Set aside to chill in the refrigerator.

Arrange the greens on a large platter, and drizzle with *Latholemono* to taste. Sprinkle with additional sea salt, if desired, and garnish with the Kalamata olives and the lemon, if desired.

YIAYIA'S TIP: After you've added the salt, taste the water to be sure it isn't too salty. While you want to have enough salt to flavor the greens, remember that you will be drinking the cooking liquid as a cleansing juice. Add more water if necessary.

Maroulosalata (mah-roo-LOH-sah-lah-TAH)

ROMAINE LETTUCE SALAD

I think romaine lettuce is often underrated. Romaine is crisp and tender, holds up well to intense flavors, and is surprisingly nutritionally dense. It has a lovely, mild flavor and pairs well with hearty main courses. In Greece, almost everything is served seasonally, and lettuce is no exception. This is a salad reminiscent of Easter, spring, and the beginning of summer.

SERVES 4 TO 6

FOR THE SALAD

2 heads romaine lettuce

6 scallions, white and soft green parts, very thinly sliced

½ cup finely chopped fresh dill

⅓ cup grated kefalotiri or Parmesan cheese (optional)

FOR THE DRESSING

2 tablespoons red wine vinegar

¼ teaspoon sea salt, plus more to taste

¼ teaspoon freshly ground black pepper, plus more to taste

3 tablespoons extra-virgin olive oil

Cut or tear the romaine into bite-size pieces, removing and discarding the particularly tough ribs. Wash the romaine in several changes of cold water and dry well. Combine the romaine, scallions, and dill in a large serving bowl.

Whisk together the vinegar, salt, and pepper in a small bowl and slowly drizzle in the olive oil while constantly whisking. Add the dressing to the salad a little at a time to taste, mixing gently as you go. If your romaine is in season and very fresh, you may not want to use all of the dressing. Sprinkle the kefalotiri or Parmesan cheese (if using) over the top of the salad and give it another quick toss. Serve immediately.

VARIATION: Want a little extra pizzazz? Halve the heads of romaine lengthwise, so that you have 4 halves. Brush with a little olive oil on all sides and throw the halves on a hot grill for 2 to 3 minutes per side or until slightly charred but still crispy. Place the romaine halves on individual plates or a large serving dish. Divide the scallions and dill evenly among the romaine halves, and drizzle with the dressing to taste. Sprinkle the cheese (if using) over the top of the romaine. Serve immediately.

Aunt Aphrodite's Beet and Apple Salad

This is one of my aunt Aphrodite's most famous and requested recipes. Simple, beautiful, and earthy, it is a great addition to any family-style meal.

SERVES 6

3 medium red beets
2 Granny Smith apples, cored, peeled, and diced
1 clove garlic, finely chopped
2 teaspoons red or white wine vinegar
½ teaspoon sea salt, plus more to taste
1¾ to 2 cups fat-free Greek yogurt, to taste
1 cup finely chopped walnuts, plus more for
    garnish

In a large pot set over medium-high heat, boil the beets in plenty of salted water for 35 to 45 minutes, depending on their size, until tender. Drain the beets and when cool enough to handle, slip the skins off and cut them into a medium dice. You may want to wear disposable plastic or latex kitchen gloves when peeling the beets to prevent the beet juice from dyeing your hands red.

In a large mixing bowl, gently mix together the beets, apples, garlic, vinegar, and salt. Add the yogurt, a little bit at a time, and gently stir together until the desired consistency is reached. Gently fold in 1 cup of the walnuts.

Taste and adjust seasonings, if necessary. Serve garnished with the remaining chopped walnuts.

THE FABULOUS ATHENS BAKER BOYS

Right near my good friend Yianni's apartment in Athens, there is an incredible bakery called *Artopita Zaharoplastiki*, owned by the Georgiadis family, which has become a neighborhood institution. It is run by a husband, wife, and son team, who, like so many families in Greece, have worked together in the family business for many years. The father, Theodoros, apprenticed under a master baker

and learned to measure his ingredients on a hundred-year-old scale. In 1996, the family opened their current bakery, where they begin their workday by baking fresh bread at 3:30 A.M., six days per week. At age eighteen, son Kostas, who is thirty today, came to work with his mom and dad and will likely continue his father's craft for decades to come.

Greeks have a true relationship with the food they eat. Nearly every morning, families buy their fresh bread and pastries at local neighborhood and village bakeries just like *Artopita Zaharoplastiki*. Customers know their bakers, who take so much pride in their craft, and everyone is clear about exactly which ingredients are in everything they buy for themselves and their families to enjoy.

Pites

SAVORY PHYLLO PASTRIES

Pita means "pie" in Greek. The most famous of the Greek *pites* are *tiropita* and *spanakopita*. However, there are dozens more classic varieties of the Greek *pites*. *Pites* are most often made with phyllo dough. There are two major varieties of phyllo in Greece, the country rustic version and the paper-thin version you find in supermarkets and specialty stores. You can make both types yourself at home, but if you are like me and are always in a rush, the store-bought phyllo is just great. In my experience, you could fill this heavenly, light, and flaky pastry with almost anything, and it would turn out delicious. However, bakers beware. When phyllo is the star of your show, she can be a real diva. If you keep phyllo waiting too long, she will get dry and brittle fast. And also, due to her wafer-thin physique, you have to handle her with kid gloves, or she will fall to pieces. Needless to say, phyllo is the most difficult cohost I've ever worked with.

A NOTE ON THE RECIPES IN THIS CHAPTER

In the interest of heart health, I recommend brushing the layers of phyllo dough with extra-virgin olive oil instead of with melted butter. Using olive oil creates lighter, more healthful dishes. Phyllo pies in Greece traditionally are made with either olive oil or melted butter, but the recipes in this chapter refer only to olive oil. If you wish to use melted butter to create a richer, heartier phyllo pie, simply use an equal amount of melted butter instead of olive oil. My mom always uses Land O'Lakes salted butter sticks. This is the only chapter in this book in which I recommend using salted butter. If you do use salted butter, reduce the amount of salt in the filling by ¼ teaspoon.

Phyllo dough dries out very quickly. Once you roll it out, keep the unused portion covered with wax paper or plastic wrap. You can also put a slightly damp kitchen towel over the wax paper or plastic wrap, as long as it does not directly touch the phyllo.

Pites are usually served hot or warm, but leftovers are equally delicious cold or reheated, packed in a picnic lunch, or straight from the fridge for breakfast or lunch!

IN THIS CHAPTER

Spanakopita *(spah-nah-KOH-pee-tah)*

SPINACH FETA PIE

I love sharing this Greek favorite with my friends. Over the years I have mastered making an excellent *spanakopita*. In fact, you'd be hard-pressed to find someone working in entertainment news in Hollywood who hasn't tried my *spanakopita* and who wouldn't agree that it's pretty darn delicious. Still, I must admit that mine will never be quite as good as my mom's. She has the magic touch. Practice makes perfect, and while Mom's is still the best, yours will be pretty fantastic too!

SERVES 8 TO 10

½ cup extra-virgin olive oil, divided, plus more
    for baking dish
1 bunch scallions, white and tender green parts,
    washed and thinly sliced
½ large sweet onion, finely chopped
2 pounds fresh spinach, coarse stems removed,
    washed in several changes of cold water,
    drained, and chopped
1 pound brine-packed Greek feta
1 cup finely chopped fresh dill
4 large eggs, beaten
¼ teaspoon freshly ground black pepper
1 (1-pound) package phyllo dough sheets
    (13 × 18 inches), thawed (see tip, page 112)

Preheat oven to 350 degrees. Oil a 9 × 13-inch baking dish.

Heat 2 tablespoons of the olive oil in a large pot over medium heat. Add the scallions and the onion, and sauté until translucent, about 5 to 6 minutes. Add the spinach and sauté until just wilted. Remove from heat, let cool slightly, and transfer to a fine-mesh strainer. Cool slightly, then squeeze as much excess water as possible from the spinach, and transfer to a large mixing bowl.

Crumble the feta into small pieces and add it to the spinach mixture. Add the dill and mix gently to combine. Add the eggs and pepper. Mix well to combine with impeccably clean hands or a silicone spatula.

Roll the phyllo dough out on a flat surface, working quickly and keeping it covered to prevent it from drying out. Place 2 phyllo sheets into the baking dish at a time, centering them and letting the edges hang over the sides. Brush the top sheet of each 2-sheet layer with a little of the remaining olive oil, but do not brush the overhanging edges. Continue in this manner until you have used 10 of the phyllo dough sheets. Spread the spinach-feta mixture evenly over the

(recipe continues)

phyllo dough layers in the prepared dish. Fold the overhanging phyllo dough over the filling, then continue to layer the phyllo dough, brushing each 2-sheet layer with olive oil, until you have used all of the dough. Trim the top layers of phyllo to fit the baking dish. Slowly pour the remaining olive oil on top, and spread evenly.

Before baking, using a large knife, very carefully score the pie into 8 to 10 pieces, cutting through the top layers just until you reach the filling. Precutting makes it much easier to serve, as the phyllo dough becomes crisp and very fragile after baking.

Bake for 50 to 60 minutes or until the top is golden brown and flaky, watching carefully. Cool for 10 minutes, slice the precut pieces all the way through, and serve.

DEBBIE'S TIP: As noted earlier, as with most of the phyllo pies, *spanakopita* can be made with either melted butter or extra-virgin olive oil. I find the olive oil version to be a lighter, more healthful dish, but I also love to indulge in my mom's decadent, traditional version once in a while. To make it Mom's way, replace the olive oil used to brush the phyllo with 6 tablespoons of melted butter (see tip, page 112), add an extra egg, and use 1½ pounds of feta instead of 1 pound. It's over-the-top delicious!

Tiropita *(tee-ROH-pee-tah)*

SAVORY CHEESE PIE

Tiropita really is the crown jewel of all the *pites.* If you like cheese, you will love this recipe. In Greece, it is typically eaten as a breakfast or a midmorning snack. But in my house, it is eaten round the clock, as it is one of my family's favorites.

SERVES 8 TO 10

6 tablespoons extra-virgin olive oil, plus more for baking dish
¾ pound brine-packed Greek feta
1 pint large-curd low-fat cottage cheese
6 large eggs
½ teaspoon freshly ground black pepper
1 (1-pound) package phyllo dough sheets (13 × 18 inches), thawed (see tip, page 112)

Preheat oven to 350 degrees. Oil a 9 × 13-inch baking dish.

In a large mixing bowl, combine the feta, cottage cheese, eggs, and pepper.

Roll the phyllo dough out on a flat surface, working quickly and keeping it covered to prevent it from drying out. Place 2 phyllo sheets into the baking dish at a time, centering them and letting the edges hang over the sides. Brush the top sheet of each 2-sheet layer with a little of the remaining olive oil, but do not brush the overhanging edges. Continue in this manner until you have used 10 of the phyllo dough sheets. Spread the cheese mixture evenly over the phyllo dough layers in the prepared dish. Fold the overhanging phyllo dough over the filling, then continue to layer the phyllo dough, brushing each 2-sheet layer with olive oil, until you have used all of the dough. Trim the top layers of phyllo to fit the baking dish. Slowly pour the remaining olive oil on top, and spread evenly.

Before baking, using a large knife, very carefully score the pie into 8 to 10 pieces, cutting through the top layers just until you reach the filling. Precutting makes it much easier to serve, as the phyllo dough becomes crisp and very fragile after baking.

Bake for 50 to 60 minutes or until the top is golden brown and flaky, watching carefully. Cool for 10 minutes, slice the precut pieces all the way through, and serve.

DEBBIE'S TIP: You can also make Savory Cheese Pies in individual, appetizer-size triangles. Follow the method for *Trigona Thessalonikis* (page 266).

Hortopita *(hor-TOH-pee-tah)*

MIXED WILD GREENS PIE

Hortopita is a truly delicious greens pie. There are many ways to prepare it, but I prefer this method, which uses the same technique as that used to make *spanakopita*. This version is lighter than the Spinach Feta Pie (page 115), and it has a deeper, earthier flavor due to the variety of greens and fresh herbs used. You can truly make this dish your own by using different combinations of herbs and greens, so get creative and have fun! For a lighter dish, omit the feta.

SERVES 8 TO 10

½ cup plus 1 tablespoon extra-virgin olive oil, divided, plus more for baking dish

1 medium yellow onion, finely chopped

6 scallions, including soft green parts, thinly sliced

3 cloves garlic, finely chopped

2 pounds greens (spinach, dandelion, and mustard), washed in several changes of cold water, drained, and roughly chopped

1 cup finely chopped fresh Italian flat-leaf parsley

½ cup finely chopped fresh dill

2 tablespoons finely chopped fresh mint

¼ teaspoon sea salt

½ teaspoon freshly ground black pepper

2 large eggs, beaten

½ pound brine-packed Greek feta, crumbled (optional)

1 (1-pound) package phyllo dough sheets (13 × 18 inches), thawed (see tip, page 112)

Preheat oven to 350 degrees. Oil a 9 × 13-inch baking dish.

Heat 3 tablespoons of the olive oil in a large sauté pan over medium heat. Add the onion and scallions, and sauté until translucent, about 5 to 6 minutes, stirring frequently. Add the garlic and sauté for 1 minute more. Reduce heat to medium-low, and, working in batches if necessary, begin adding handfuls of the greens to the sauté pan. Sauté the greens until they cook down and become soft, adding more greens as space becomes available, about 10 to 12 minutes. Add the parsley and cook for 2 minutes more. Remove from heat, cool slightly, and then squeeze as much water as possible from the greens.

Transfer the cooked greens mixture to a large mixing bowl and stir in the dill, mint, salt, pepper, and beaten eggs. Gently fold in the crumbled feta (if using), so that it keeps a relatively chunky texture. Set aside.

Roll the phyllo dough out on a flat surface, working quickly and keeping it covered to prevent it from drying out. Place 2 phyllo sheets into the baking dish at a time, centering them and letting the edges hang over the sides. Brush the top sheet of each 2-sheet layer with a little of the remaining olive oil, but do not brush the overhanging edges. Continue in this manner until you have used 10 of the phyllo dough sheets. Spread the greens mixture evenly over the phyllo dough layers in the prepared dish. Fold the overhanging phyllo dough over the filling, then continue to layer the phyllo dough on top of the greens, brushing each 2-sheet layer with olive oil until you have used the full pound of the phyllo dough. Trim the edges of the top layers to fit the baking dish. Slowly pour the remaining olive oil on top, and spread evenly.

Before baking, using a large knife, very carefully score the pie into 8 to 10 pieces, cutting through the top layers just until you reach the filling. Precutting makes it much easier to serve, as the phyllo dough becomes crisp and very fragile after baking.

Bake for 50 to 60 minutes or until the top is golden brown and flaky, watching carefully. Cool for 10 minutes, slice the precut pieces all the way through, and serve.

Kolokithopita *(koh-loh-kee-THOH-pee-tah)*

ZUCCHINI AND SUMMER SQUASH PIE

As you may have noticed from the multitude of zucchini recipes in this book, zucchini is one of the most widely used vegetables in Greece, and it is definitely one of my favorites! Since zucchini is a bit of chameleon and takes on the flavors of whatever is around it, the savory and fresh herbs in this *pita* really shine. The mint gives it a nice and refreshing note.

SERVES 6 TO 8

1 pound zucchini, ends sliced off and discarded

1 pound yellow summer squash (if unavailable, use 2 pounds zucchini total), ends sliced off and discarded

½ teaspoon sea salt

½ cup plus 1 tablespoon extra-virgin olive oil, divided, plus more for baking dish

2 medium yellow onions, finely chopped

1 bunch scallions, white and soft green parts, thinly sliced

½ cup finely chopped fresh Italian flat-leaf parsley

3 tablespoons finely chopped fresh mint

3 large eggs, beaten

½ teaspoon freshly ground black pepper

½ pound brine-packed Greek feta, crumbled

1 (1-pound) package phyllo dough sheets (13 × 18 inches), thawed (see tip, page 112)

Coarsely grate the zucchini and summer squash, mix together in a colander, and use your impeccably clean hands to squeeze as much water as possible from the mixture. Toss with the salt and set the colander over a large bowl. Set a small plate on top of the zucchini mixture, and put a weight (such as a large can of tomatoes) on top of the plate to help squeeze out more water. Set aside for 30 to 60 minutes, then squeeze again one last time to remove any excess water.

Preheat oven to 350 degrees. Oil a 9 × 13-inch baking dish.

Heat 3 tablespoons of the olive oil in a large sauté pan over medium heat. Add the onion and scallion and sauté until translucent, about 5 to 6 minutes, stirring frequently. Remove the onion mixture from the heat and let cool slightly. In a large mixing bowl, combine the onion mixture with the drained zucchini and squash, parsley, mint, eggs, and pepper. Gently stir to combine. Carefully fold in the feta so that it keeps a relatively chunky texture. Set aside.

Roll the phyllo dough out on a flat surface, working quickly and keeping it covered to prevent it from drying out. Place 2 phyllo sheets into the baking dish at a time, centering them and letting the edges hang over the sides. Brush the top sheet of each 2-sheet layer with a little of the remaining olive oil, but do not brush the overhanging edges. Continue in this manner until you have used 10 of the phyllo dough sheets. Spread the zucchini-squash mixture evenly over the phyllo dough layers in the prepared dish. Fold the overhanging phyllo dough over the filling, then continue to layer the phyllo dough, brushing each 2-sheet layer with olive oil, until you have used all of the dough. Trim the top layers of phyllo to fit the baking dish. Slowly pour the remaining olive oil on top, and spread evenly.

Before baking, using a large knife, very carefully score the pie into 8 to 10 pieces, cutting through the top layers just until you reach the filling. Precutting makes it much easier to serve, as the phyllo dough becomes crisp and very fragile after baking.

Bake for 50 to 60 minutes or until the top is golden brown and flaky, watching carefully. Cool for 10 minutes, slice the precut pieces all the way through, and serve.

Kotopita *(koh-TOH-pee-tah)*

CHICKEN PIE

This is the Greek version of chicken pot pie. Comforting and delicious, it is a great way to turn leftover chicken into something scrumptious and new. I like to make this phyllo pie with herb-roasted chicken, so I often double the recipe when I make *Perfect Herb-Roasted Chicken and Vegetables* (page 210), or I just pick up an herbed rotisserie chicken on the way home from work for a quick supper.

SERVES 8

½ cup plus 1 tablespoon extra-virgin olive oil, divided, plus more for baking dish

1 recipe *Perfect Herb-Roasted Chicken and Vegetables* (page 210) *or* other roasted chicken

2 medium yellow onions, diced

1 bunch scallions, white and green parts, thinly sliced

1 tablespoon dried oregano

½ cup fresh Italian flat-leaf parsley, chopped, plus more for garnish

¼ cup chopped fresh dill

3 large eggs, beaten

1 cup kefalotiri or Parmesan cheese, grated

½ teaspoon sea salt

½ teaspoon freshly ground black pepper

1 (1-pound) package phyllo dough sheets (13 × 18 inches), thawed (see tip, page 112)

Preheat oven to 350 degrees. Grease a 9 × 13-inch baking dish. Remove and discard skin and bones from chicken, and shred the meat into small pieces (about 4 cups). Set aside.

Heat 3 tablespoons of the olive oil in a large sauté pan over medium heat. Add the onions, scallions, and oregano, and sauté until the onions are translucent, about 5 to 6 minutes, stirring frequently. Add the parsley and cook for 1 minute more. Remove from heat and add the dill. Add the onion mixture to the chicken and fold together. Stir in the eggs and kefalotiri or Parmesan cheese along with the salt and pepper. Set aside.

Roll the phyllo dough out on a flat surface, working quickly and keeping it covered to prevent it from drying out. Place 2 phyllo sheets into the baking dish at a time, centering them and letting the edges hang over the sides. Brush the top sheet of each 2-sheet layer with a little of the remaining olive oil, but do not brush the overhanging edges. Continue in this manner until you have used 10 of the phyllo dough sheets. Spread the chicken mixture evenly over the phyllo dough layers in the prepared dish. Fold the overhanging phyllo dough over the filling, then continue to layer the phyllo dough, brushing each 2-sheet layer with olive oil, until you have used all of the dough. Trim the top layers of phyllo to fit the baking dish. Slowly pour the remaining olive oil on top, and spread evenly.

Before baking, using a large knife, very carefully score the pie into 8 to 10 pieces, cutting through the top layers just until you reach the filling. Precutting makes it much easier to serve, as the phyllo dough becomes crisp and very fragile after baking.

Bake for 50 to 60 minutes or until the top is golden brown and flaky, watching carefully. Cool for 10 minutes, slice the precut pieces all the way through, and serve.

DEBBIE'S TIP: *Kotopita* is truly versatile and is equally as delicious when made with ground chicken. Simply substitute 1½ pounds of ground chicken for the roasted chicken. Add the raw ground chicken to the translucent onions, scallions, and oregano in the sauté pan. Sauté the chicken until it slightly browned and just cooked through. Continue with the recipe as written. Using ground chicken can create an even more moist final product, so try it both ways and see which you and your family prefer!

Kreatopita (kreh-ah-TOH-pee-tah)

EXQUISITE SAVORY MEAT PIE

Kreatopita is just so darn good! The way all of these ingredients come together is out-of-this-world delicious. This was always my dad's favorite, too. Yummy!

SERVES 8 TO 10

½ cup plus 1 tablespoon extra-virgin olive oil, divided, plus more for baking dish

3 large leeks, halved lengthwise, washed well and dried, white and soft green parts separated and thinly sliced (see tip, page 29)

1 large yellow onion, chopped

¼ cup water

1½ pounds ground lamb or ground beef (85 percent lean)

2 teaspoons sea salt

½ teaspoon freshly ground black pepper

½ cup chopped fresh Italian flat-leaf parsley

1 teaspoon dried oregano

1 to 2 tablespoons chopped fresh mint, to taste

1 large egg, lightly beaten

1 (1-pound) package phyllo dough sheets (13 × 18 inches), thawed (see tip, page 112)

Preheat oven to 350 degrees. Oil a 9 × 13 inch baking dish.

Heat 1½ tablespoons of the olive oil in a large Dutch oven or stockpot over medium heat. Add the white parts of the leeks, and then the onion, sauté until translucent, about 5 to 6 minutes, and set aside. Meanwhile, in a large sauté pan, heat another 1½ tablespoons of olive oil over medium heat. Add the green parts of the leeks, and cook, stirring frequently, for 2 minutes. Slowly stir in the water, and cook for 4 to 5 minutes more.

Transfer the green parts and any remaining liquid from the sauté pan into the pot with the onions. Stir to combine and set the pot back over medium heat. Add the meat along with the salt, pepper, parsley, oregano, and mint, and cook for about 5 to 7 minutes, until the meat is browned and no longer pink, stirring constantly. Remove from heat and set aside to cool slightly. Slowly stir in the beaten egg. Drain off and discard the excess liquid.

Roll the phyllo dough out on a flat surface, working quickly and keeping it covered to prevent it from drying out. Place 2 phyllo sheets into the baking dish at a time, centering them and letting the edges hang over the sides. Brush the top sheet of each 2-sheet layer with a little of the remaining olive oil, but do not brush the overhanging edges. Continue in this manner until you have used 10 of the phyllo dough sheets. Spread all of the meat mixture evenly over the phyllo dough layers in the prepared dish. Fold the overhanging phyllo dough over the filling, then continue to layer the phyllo dough, brushing each 2-sheet layer with olive oil, until you have used all of the dough. Trim the top layers of phyllo to fit the baking dish. Slowly pour the remaining olive oil on top, and spread evenly.

Before baking, using a large knife, very carefully score the pie into 8 to 10 pieces, cutting through the top layers just until you reach the filling. Precutting makes it much easier to serve, as the phyllo dough becomes crisp and very fragile after baking.

Bake for 50 to 60 minutes or until the top is golden brown and flaky, watching carefully. Cool for 10 minutes, slice the precut pieces all the way through, and serve.

Prasopita *(prah-SOH-pee-tah)*

LEEK AND CHEESE PIE

Leeks are harvested and eaten in the wintertime in Greece, and so this *pita* is served during the colder months. If you've never had leeks before, they taste like very mildly flavored onions. They also have a prominent place in Greek mythology. It is said that leeks were included in ritual offerings to Leto, the mother of the twin Greek gods Apollo and Artemis, because she craved them during her pregnancy. Today, when the winter months roll around, I also crave this leek-stuffed phyllo pie. It has a light and airy texture with a very sophisticated and delicate flavor.

SERVES 8

½ cup plus 2 tablespoons extra-virgin olive oil, divided

2 pounds leeks, halved lengthwise, washed well and dried, white and soft green parts separated and thinly sliced (see tip, page 29)

½ cup chopped fresh Italian flat-leaf parsley

2 tablespoons finely chopped fresh mint

4 large eggs

½ pound Greek mizithra *or* ricotta cheese

½ teaspoon sea salt

½ teaspoon freshly ground black pepper

½ pound brine-packed Greek feta, crumbled

1 (1-pound) package phyllo dough sheets (13 × 18 inches), thawed (see tip, page 112)

Preheat oven to 350 degrees. Oil a 9 × 13-inch baking dish.

Set 2 large sauté pans over medium-high heat. Add 2 tablespoons of the olive oil to each pan. Add the white parts of the leeks to one pan and the green parts to the other pan, cooking the white parts for 6 minutes, or until translucent, and the green parts for 8 minutes, or until tender, stirring both frequently. After 6 minutes, add the parsley to the pan with the white parts of the leeks and cook for 1 minute more. Transfer both parts of the leeks to a large mixing bowl, and add the mint.

In a separate medium mixing bowl, whisk the eggs together with the mizithra or ricotta cheese. Add the egg and cheese mixture to the leeks, along with the salt and pepper, and stir to combine. Gently fold in the feta crumbles so that they keep a relatively chunky texture. Set aside.

Roll the phyllo dough out on a flat surface, working quickly and keeping it covered to prevent it from drying out. Place 2 phyllo sheets into the baking dish at a time, centering them and letting the edges hang over the sides. Brush the top sheet of each 2-sheet layer with a little of the remaining olive oil, but do not brush the overhanging edges. Continue in this manner until you have used 10 of the phyllo dough sheets. Spread the leek mixture evenly over the phyllo dough layers in the prepared dish. Fold the overhanging phyllo dough over the filling, then continue to layer the phyllo dough, brushing each 2-sheet layer with olive oil, until you have used all of the dough. Trim the top layers of phyllo to fit the baking dish. Slowly pour the remaining olive oil on top, and spread evenly.

Before baking, using a large knife, very carefully score the pie into 8 to 10 pieces, cutting through the top layers just until you reach the filling. Precutting makes it much easier to serve, as the phyllo dough becomes crisp and very fragile after baking.

Bake for 50 to 60 minutes or until the top is golden brown and flaky, watching carefully. Cool for 10 minutes, slice the precut pieces all the way through, and serve.

Soupes kai Stifathes
SOUPS, STEWS, AND ONE-POT MEALS

Soups and stews are staples of Greek cuisine. Packed with protein and classic aromatic seasonings, they are just fantastic. I call many of these simmered delights one-pot meals because I often serve them along with chunks of crusty bread and a family-style salad for an easy and nourishing supper. One of things I love most about cooking up a big pot of soup is that it fills the whole house with a lovely aroma that is very nostalgic for me. Who doesn't love to come home to a house where a fragrant savory soup has been simmering all day on the stove, especially in the fall or winter?

Faki (fah-KEE)

GREEK LENTIL SOUP

This Greek twist on lentil soup is fast, easy, and oh so good. Lentils are a great source of inexpensive protein, and they're packed full of immune system–boosting vitamins.

SERVES 6 TO 8

½ cup extra-virgin olive oil

1 medium onion, diced

2 stalks celery, diced

3 large carrots, peeled and diced

2 teaspoons sea salt

1 teaspoon freshly ground pepper

1 clove garlic, finely chopped

1 tablespoon tomato paste

1 pound brown lentils, picked over, rinsed very well, and drained

8 cups water

2 bay leaves

1 small fresh hot red chili pepper (seeded if desired), diced, or ¼ teaspoon crushed red pepper flakes (optional)

Red wine vinegar (optional, for serving)

Heat the olive oil in a large stockpot or Dutch oven set over medium heat. Add the onion, celery, carrots, salt, and pepper, and sauté until the onion is translucent but not browned, about 5 to 6 minutes, stirring frequently. Stir in the garlic and cook 1 minute more. Stir in the tomato paste.

Add the lentils, water, bay leaves, and chili pepper or pepper flakes (if using). Bring to a boil over medium-high heat. Reduce heat to low, cover, and simmer for about 45 minutes, until the lentils are tender.

Taste and adjust seasonings, if necessary. Traditionally, 1 tablespoon of red wine vinegar is added to each bowl just before serving.

Magiritsa *(mah-ghee-REE-tsah)*

GREEK EASTER SOUP

Magiritsa is an institution in Greece. In fact, I don't think you can celebrate Easter in Greece without serving some form of this classic soup, which, by the way, I adore! As I've mentioned before, the Greeks despise wasting anything, so the traditional version of this soup uses leftover lamb parts, such as intestines, lungs, and hearts. I prefer to use lamb shoulder, which is a more accessible cut of meat for most of my non-Greek friends. However, in keeping with tradition, I do use leftover lamb bones to make the stock.

SERVES 6 TO 8

1 bunch dill

2 bay leaves

1 bunch fresh Italian flat-leaf parsley, with stems

10 cloves garlic, smashed and peeled

10 whole black peppercorns

3 tablespoons extra-virgin olive oil

2 medium yellow onions, diced

2¼ teaspoons sea salt, divided

2 celery stalks, chopped into 2-inch chunks

3 carrots, peeled and chopped into
2-inch chunks

3 quarts water

1 teaspoon freshly ground black pepper

3 pounds lamb shoulder, whole with
bones intact, trimmed of fat

2½ pounds lamb bones

3 scallions, white and soft green parts,
thinly sliced

½ cup long-grain white rice

1 recipe *Avgolemono* (page 70), made with
the broth from the soup

2 heads romaine lettuce, shredded

Make a bouquet garni for the broth: Separate the dill stems from the fronds. Finely chop ¾ cup dill fronds and set aside. Cut a large piece of cheesecloth, about 8 inches square. Place the bay leaves, parsley, dill stems, garlic, and peppercorns inside the cheesecloth, bring the ends up, and tie it tightly into a pouch with some kitchen twine. Set aside.

Heat the olive oil in a large stockpot or Dutch oven over medium heat. Add the onions and ¼ teaspoon of the salt, and sauté until the onions are translucent and very soft, about 6 to 7 minutes, stirring frequently. Stir in the celery and carrots, coating them in the oil, and cook for another 2 minutes. Pour in the water, and scrape up any brown bits stuck to the sides of the pot. Increase heat to medium-high, and bring to a boil. Reduce heat to simmer.

Rub the remaining 2 teaspoons of salt and the ground pepper all over the lamb shoulder to season it. Gently submerge the lamb shoulder and the lamb bones in the water along with the bouquet garni. Increase heat to medium-high, and return the mixture to a boil. Reduce heat to low, and simmer the broth, uncovered, for 2 hours or until the lamb meat is very tender. Skim the surface with a large metal spoon every so often to remove any foam or froth that floats to the top.

Gently lift out the cooked lamb shoulder, and transfer it to a large platter to cool. Remove and discard the bones and the bouquet garni. Strain the broth through a fine metal sieve into a large, clean stockpot or Dutch oven, and discard the vegetables and any other solids that remain in the sieve.

When the lamb shoulder is cool enough to handle, pull the meat off the bones and chop into bite-size pieces. Discard the bones, and add the chopped, cooked lamb back into the broth. Bring the soup to a boil over medium-high heat, then reduce to a simmer. Add the scallions and rice and continue to simmer until the rice is cooked, about 20 minutes, stirring occasionally. Remove from heat.

Make the *Avgolemono*, using the hot broth from this recipe as the broth for the sauce.

Slowly stir the sauce into the remaining soup, making sure to mix well so as not to scramble the eggs. Do not boil the soup again after the *Avgolemono* has been added. Remove from heat, and add the fresh dill.

Taste and adjust seasonings, if necessary. Serve warm in individual serving bowls, generously garnished with the shredded romaine lettuce.

Hirino me Prassa *(hee-ree-NOH meh PRAH-sah)*

PORK AND LEEK STEW

This a great example of a classic and comforting Greek wintertime stew. In Greece, produce is available seasonally only. Cool-weather vegetables such as leeks show up in the late fall and, for me, are truly one of the best treats of winter. For a hearty winter feast, serve this stew on a bed of *Kritharaki me Domata kai Feta* (page 180).

SERVES 4 TO 6

1½ pounds leeks, halved lengthwise, white and tender green parts cut into 2-inch pieces and washed (see tip, page 29)

1½ pounds boneless pork shoulder, cut into 6 large pieces of equal size

1 tablespoon sea salt, plus more to taste

1½ teaspoons freshly ground black pepper

½ cup extra-virgin olive oil

2 medium yellow onions, chopped

1 tablespoon tomato paste diluted in 3 cups water

Bring a generous amount of salted water to a boil over high heat in a large stockpot or Dutch oven with a tight-fitting lid, and boil the leeks for 6 minutes. Drain the leeks in a fine-mesh colander, rinse with cold water, and set aside. Empty the pot and wipe it clean with a paper towel or clean dishtowel.

Season the pork with the salt and pepper. In the pot used to boil the leeks, heat the olive oil over medium-high heat. Add the pork and brown on all sides, about 10 minutes. Stir in the onions, reduce heat to medium, and cook until the onions are translucent, 5 to 6 minutes. Slowly pour the tomato paste–water mixture into the pot, being sure to scrape up any brown bits that may be stuck to the pot. Increase heat to medium-high and bring to a boil. Reduce heat to medium-low, cover, and cook until the meat is tender and sauce has thickened, about 1 hour, stirring occasionally. Add the leeks and cook for another 20 minutes. Remove from heat. Allow the stew to cool slightly, and serve.

———————— 🇬🇷 ————————

DEBBIE'S TIP: If you serve *Hirino me Prassa,* or any other hearty stew, over *Kritharaki me Domata kai Feta,* omit the feta cheese. Otherwise, the dish will be too rich and the flavors will not marry well.

Hortosoupa (hor-TOH-soo-pah)

CLASSIC GREEK VEGETABLE SOUP

This rustic puréed soup is a real feast for the taste buds. It's perfect on a cold, snowy winter's day. On snow days, when school was canceled, all the neighborhood kids would pile into my mom's kitchen after a day spent sledding and having snowball fights for a hot bowl of this hearty soup. Serve with a hunk of *Uncle Dimitri's Homemade Bread* (page 277) or *Easy Baked Croutons* (page 273) for an extra treat.

SERVES 4 TO 6

8 cups water

4 medium russet potatoes, peeled and diced

2 medium yellow onions, finely chopped

1 celery stalk with leaves, finely chopped

4 to 5 carrots, peeled and finely chopped

1 tablespoon sea salt

¼ cup extra-virgin olive oil

5 ripe medium tomatoes

½ teaspoon freshly ground black pepper

1 recipe *Easy Baked Croutons* (page 273) *or* 1 loaf *Uncle Dimitri's Homemade Bread* (page 277) (optional)

Add the water, potatoes, onions, celery, carrots, salt, and olive oil to a large stockpot. Bring to a boil over medium-high heat, reduce heat to medium, and continue to simmer for 20 minutes, uncovered, until the vegetables are tender.

Poke the tomatoes in a few spots with the tines of a fork and add them to the pot. Reduce heat to low, cover, and simmer for 45 minutes more.

Stir in the pepper, then transfer soup in batches to a blender or food processor. Blend until smooth (see tip). Ladle the soup into individual serving bowls and serve with croutons or bread (if using).

YIAYIA'S TIP: Never fill your blender or food processor more than halfway with hot liquids. If the machine is too full, the escaping steam can force the top off and spray hot liquid all over you and your kitchen. Cover the top with a clean kitchen towel before you turn the machine on, work slowly, and take care not to burn yourself.

Fasolatha *(fah-soh-LAH-thah)*

NAVY BEAN SOUP

My mom used to make this Greek winter staple for the whole family and all our friends in the wintertime. After a cold afternoon at track practice, I couldn't wait to get home and sit down to this meal, complete with Mom's amazing, fresh-from-the-oven homemade bread and her homemade pickled vegetables. Just like Mom, you'll want to pass some vinegar at the table to give the soup a little tang. Balsamic vinegar will interfere with the flavor of the soup, though, so I recommend you save it for your favorite salad and use red or white wine vinegar or, my favorite, apple cider vinegar. The flavor of this soup improves over time, and it freezes well, so don't worry about making too much.

SERVES 6 TO 8

1 pound navy beans, picked over, rinsed very well, and drained

14 cups water, divided, plus more for soaking beans

½ cup extra-virgin olive oil

2 cloves garlic, finely chopped

1 large sweet onion, chopped

3 stalks celery, diced, leaves included

3 carrots, peeled and diced

1 small fresh hot red chili pepper (seeded if desired), finely chopped, *or* ⅛ to ¼ teaspoon crushed red pepper flakes

¼ cup tomato paste, plus more to taste

2 teaspoons sea salt, plus more to taste

½ teaspoon freshly ground black pepper

Red wine, white wine, or apple cider vinegar, to taste (optional)

Soak the beans overnight in enough water to cover by 2 inches. Drain and rinse well. Add the beans plus 7 cups of the water to a large stockpot and bring to a boil over high heat. At the same time, heat the remaining 7 cups of water in a separate large stockpot over high heat. After the pot of water with beans in it comes to a boil, a frothy, fluffy layer of foam will rise to the top. Allow the beans to boil for 2 to 3 minutes. Drain the beans again, discarding the foamy water, and transfer the beans to the other pot of hot water. Return to a boil. This process allows some of the gases to escape, making the beans easier to digest. It also makes this soup much lighter than other bean dishes.

Add the olive oil, garlic, onion, celery, and carrots to the beans, and reduce heat to low. Cover and simmer for 1 to 1½ hours, or until beans are very tender, stirring occasionally. Add the chili pepper or pepper flakes (if using), tomato paste, salt, and pepper. Cover and simmer for another 25 to 30 minutes.

Taste and adjust seasonings, if necessary. Serve hot, garnishing each bowl with a spoonful of vinegar (if using).

DEBBIE'S TIP: Greek folk wisdom tells us always to use a wooden spoon, not metal, if you want to cook perfect, tender beans. Of course, I'm not a scientist and neither is my mom, who taught me this trick, but these are lessons that are passed down from generation to generation. You also can make this soup with cannellini beans, and it will be just as fabulous!

Enjoying an afternoon ouzo on the house in Palia Poli (the old city of Athens) with local restaurateurs. Love that Greek *philotimo!*

Kotosoupa Avgolemono *(koh-TOH-soo-pah ah-VGHO-leh-moh-noh)*

GREEK CHICKEN SOUP

Not only is this chicken soup super delicious, it is believed to have magical curative powers. My mom, along with every other Greek mother I know, refers to this delicious soup as Greek penicillin. I have to be honest with you—it really does the trick! Give it a try, especially if you're not feeling well.

SERVES 6

1 whole chicken, about 4 pounds, skin removed

12 cups water

1 onion, peeled and cut into quarters

2 teaspoons sea salt

¾ teaspoon freshly ground black pepper

2 bay leaves

½ cup long-grain white rice or orzo

1 recipe *Avgolemono* (page 70), made with the
   broth from the soup

Rinse the chicken very well, inside and out, under cold water. Add the 12 cups of water, chicken, onion, salt, pepper, and bay leaves to a large stockpot. Bring to a boil over medium-high heat. With a large metal spoon, skim off any foam or froth that rises to the top. When foam stops rising to the top, reduce heat to low and simmer, partially covered, until the chicken is falling off the bone, about 1½ hours.

Remove the chicken from the pot and set aside to cool.

Strain the broth through a fine-mesh sieve into a large bowl and discard any remaining solids. Return the strained broth to the pot and return it to a boil over medium-high heat. Stir in the rice or orzo, reduce heat to medium, and simmer, uncovered, until tender, about 15 to 20 minutes.

Meanwhile, remove the chicken meat from the bones, and shred it into small pieces. Return the shredded chicken to the pot and reduce heat to medium-low. Simmer the soup until the chicken is warmed through. Remove from heat.

Make the *Avgolemono*, using the broth from the chicken soup as the broth for the sauce.

Slowly stir the sauce back into the remaining chicken broth, mixing well so as not to scramble the eggs. Do not boil again after the sauce has been added. Add the shredded chicken.

Taste and adjust seasonings, if necessary. Serve immediately.

Fava *(FAH-vah)*

YELLOW SPLIT PEA SOUP

Fava is one of those magical comfort foods my mom would make for me whenever I needed a little pick-me-up. It has only a few select, inexpensive ingredients, yet when you taste it it's just perfect. It's vegan, so Greek families serve it often during the Lenten (fasting) seasons. Be sure your split peas are fresh. Older peas that have been exposed to oxygen for long periods (like those in bulk bins) can take much longer to cook. If you can't find yellow split peas you can substitute green split peas. The soup will be just as delicious.

SERVES 8

1 pound (about 2 cups) yellow split peas, picked over, rinsed very well, and drained

14½ cups water, divided, plus more for soaking, and as needed

½ cup extra-virgin olive oil, plus more for garnish

2 teaspoons sea salt, plus more to taste

⅓ cup finely chopped fresh Italian flat-leaf parsley, plus more for garnish

2 medium yellow onions, chopped

2 lemons cut into wedges, for garnish

Soak the peas for 1 hour in enough water to cover by 2 inches. Drain and rinse well. Place the soaked split peas in a large stockpot, add 7 cups of the water, stir to combine, and bring to a boil, uncovered, over medium-high heat. Boil for 10 minutes, stirring occasionally and skimming off the frothy foam that floats to the surface. Remove from heat, drain, and rinse well.

Return the split peas to the pot, add the remaining 7½ cups of water, and return to a boil, uncovered, over medium-high heat. Once the water begins to boil, set a timer for 30 minutes. Skim off any more foam that floats to the top. When the foam subsides, add the olive oil, salt, parsley, and onions, and stir to combine. Continue to boil over medium-high heat, stirring frequently. After 30 minutes, reduce heat to medium and cook at a high simmer, uncovered, stirring often, until the peas break down and the soup becomes creamy, almost like pudding, about 30 to 45 minutes. You may need to add a little more water, ¼ cup at a time, if the soup becomes too thick. Toward the end of cooking, the peas should be just even with the top of the water. As the soup becomes very thick, be sure to stir constantly to avoid scorching the bottom.

Taste and adjust seasonings, if necessary. Serve garnished with the chopped parsley, a drizzle of olive oil, and a wedge of lemon on the side.

DEBBIE'S TIP: You can add a splash of vinegar instead of the lemon if you'd prefer. Either way, it's delicious. As the soup cools, it will become even thicker. To reheat, just add some water until it is the consistency you like it.

Octopothi Stifado *(octo-POH-thee stee-FAH-thoh)*

OCTOPUS ONION STEW

Octopus looks like a creature from another planet, yet it tastes amazing when cooked properly, like a more tender version of lobster. Cooking octopus is a surprisingly simple process. It's true that octopus need to be cleaned of eyes, guts, beaks, and ink sacs, but don't let that scare you. Simply ask your fishmonger to do the heavy lifting and clean your octopus. When you get home, all you have to do is rinse it off under cold water and dive into making some stew. So be bold! Be brave! Make some octopus stew tonight!

SERVES 6 TO 8

12 cups water, plus more as needed

1 cup plus 2 tablespoons extra-virgin olive oil

2 (1½-pound) octopuses, cleaned and gutted, with eyes, beak, and ink sac removed (see tip, page 67)

3½ pounds shallots, peeled, ends trimmed and sliced into thirds

3 cloves garlic, minced

1¼ cups red wine

2 bay leaves

1½ teaspoons sea salt, plus more to taste

½ teaspoon freshly ground black pepper

1 whole sprig fresh rosemary

5 ripe medium tomatoes, peeled and diced

½ cup red wine vinegar

3 tablespoons chopped fresh Italian flat-leaf parsley

1 loaf crusty bread (optional)

Bring 12 cups of the water to a boil in a large stockpot set over high heat. Stir in 2 tablespoons of the olive oil and submerge the octopuses in the boiling water. When the water returns to a boil, boil the octopuses, uncovered, for 30 minutes. Drain and let cool. When the octopuses are cool enough to handle, run them under cold water, and rub off the dark outer skin. (If you cannot get it all off, don't worry!) Use a large, very sharp kitchen knife to cut the tentacles and the center section into 1½-inch chunks. Set aside.

Heat the olive oil in a large stockpot or Dutch oven set over medium heat. Add the shallots and the octopus and sauté until the shallots are translucent, about 5 to 7 minutes. Add the garlic and cook for 1 minute more. Stir in the wine, scraping up any brown bits. Then add the bay leaves, salt, pepper, and rosemary. Continue to cook for another 5 minutes, until the wine has reduced by about half. Stir in the tomatoes and cook for 1 to 2 minutes, until they start to break down. Add the vinegar, increase heat to medium-high, and bring to a boil. Reduce heat to low, cover, and simmer for 50 to 60 minutes, or until the octopus is tender. Remove from heat, stir in the parsley, cover again, and let the stew rest for 10 minutes.

If desired, slice the bread into 1-inch-thick slices and put one slice into each individual serving bowl. Ladle the stew over the bread in the bowls, and serve immediately.

Psarosoupa *(psah-ROH-soo-pah)*

FISH SOUP WITH TOMATO

Psarosoupa is a meal in itself that can be enjoyed year-round. Although it is light and simple, it is surprisingly flavorful and satisfying.

SERVES 4 TO 6

7 cups of water, divided

4 stalks celery, finely chopped

4 carrots, peeled and finely chopped

3 medium yellow onions, finely chopped

3 ripe medium tomatoes, peeled and cut into large chunks

¾ cup extra-virgin olive oil

1½ teaspoons sea salt, plus more to taste

½ teaspoon freshly ground black pepper

1¾ pounds whitefish (such as cod, grouper, or red snapper), scaled, cleaned, and cut into large, skin-on fillets

5 tablespoons long-grain white rice

Add 6 cups of the water, celery, carrots, and onions to a large stockpot, and bring to a boil over medium-high heat. Reduce heat to medium-low, and simmer for 15 minutes, uncovered. Add the tomatoes, and simmer for 45 minutes more.

Stir in the olive oil, salt, and pepper, then gently add the fish. Reduce heat to low and simmer for 15 minutes, being careful not to overcook the fish. Remove the pot from the heat, carefully lift out the fish, and transfer it to a large dish. Set aside to cool.

Strain the soup through a fine-mesh sieve into a large bowl, discarding any remaining solids, and making sure there are no stray bones in the broth. Return the broth to the pot. Add the rice and the remaining 1 cup of water. Bring to a boil over medium-high heat, stir once, reduce heat to low, cover, and simmer for 15 minutes, until the rice is done. Remove from heat.

Meanwhile, carefully peel the skin off the fish and break the fish into large chunks, again watching for and removing any residual bones. When the rice is tender, add the fish pieces back to the soup. Serve immediately.

Tahinosoupa *(tah-hee-NOH-soo-pah)*

TAHINI SOUP

Tahinosoupa is a delicious tahini soup traditionally served during Lent. It contains no meat and no dairy, and it is great any time of the year.

SERVES 6

3 tablespoons extra-virgin olive oil
2 medium yellow onions, diced
3 carrots, scrubbed clean and diced
2 stalks celery with leaves, diced
1 cup long-grain white rice
8 cups water, divided
2 tablespoons finely chopped fresh Italian
    flat-leaf parsley
1 teaspoon sea salt, plus more to taste
½ teaspoon freshly ground black pepper
1 cup tahini (sesame seed paste)
¼ cup freshly squeezed lemon juice (about
    2 lemons)

Heat the olive oil in a large stockpot or Dutch oven set over medium heat. Add the onions, carrots, and celery, and sauté until the onions are translucent and the carrots and celery are very tender, about 8 to 10 minutes, stirring frequently. Stir in the rice, coating it in the oil, and cook, stirring constantly, until it is an opaque white, about 2 minutes. (Do not brown.) Slowly pour in 7½ cups of the water, and stir in the parsley, salt, and pepper. Increase heat to medium-high, and bring to a boil. Reduce heat to low, cover, and simmer for 20 minutes.

Meanwhile, whisk together the tahini, remaining ½ cup of water, and lemon juice in a medium mixing bowl. Remove the soup from the heat and slowly add about 1 cup of the hot rice mixture to the tahini mixture to temper it, stirring vigorously to combine. Then slowly stir the tempered tahini mixture back into the hot soup.

Taste and adjust seasonings, if necessary. Serve immediately.

Youvarlakia Avgolemono *(yoo-var-LAH-kee-ah ah-VGHO-leh-moh-noh)*

GREEK MEATBALL SOUP

This seemingly simple dish is absolutely scrumptious! The *Avgolemono* acts as a soup in this recipe, making it a great way to warm your belly on a cold winter night. Serve it with *Lahanosalata* (page 94) for a perfect pairing.

SERVES 4

1 pound lean ground beef *or* lean ground turkey, chicken, or lamb

½ cup long-grain white rice, rinsed well and drained

½ cup coarsely grated onion

3 tablespoons finely chopped fresh Italian flat-leaf parsley

2 large eggs, separated

1½ teaspoons sea salt

½ teaspoon freshly ground black pepper

½ cup extra-virgin olive oil

4 to 6 cups hot water, plus more as needed

6 tablespoons freshly squeezed lemon juice (2 to 3 lemons)

Gently combine the meat, rice, onion, parsley, egg whites, salt, and pepper in a large mixing bowl with a large fork or impeccably clean hands. Mix until just combined but do not overwork, or your meatballs will be tough. Using your hands, gently form the mixture into balls about the size of a walnut.

Heat the olive oil in a large pot set over medium heat. Gently place the meatballs into the oil, arranging them in neat rows. Slowly pour 4 cups of the hot water over the meatballs to cover, using more water if necessary. Increase heat to medium-high, bring to a boil, and reduce heat to low. Simmer for 40 minutes or until the meatballs are tender and fully cooked. Add more water if less than 1 cup remains. You should end up with about 2 cups of broth in the pot when the meat is done.

Whisk the 2 egg yolks in a medium mixing bowl until smooth, then slowly whisk in the lemon juice. Temper the egg mixture by slowly pouring 1 cup of hot broth from the pot into the egg yolk mixture, whisking continuously until well combined. Slowly pour the egg yolk–broth mixture back into the pot with the meatballs, stirring gently to combine. Do not allow the broth to boil at this point or the eggs will scramble.

Gently shake the pot to coat the meatballs. Continue to cook over low heat, stirring constantly, until slightly thickened, 2 to 3 minutes. Serve immediately, with plenty of crusty bread to soak up the sauce.

Psaria
SEAFOOD MAIN DISHES

The Greek coastline, over 8,000 miles long along with over 1,400 islands, coupled with its geographical location across the Mediterranean, Aegean, and Ionian Seas, is any fisherman's dream. There is an abundance of seafood in Greece, with over 250 edible varieties in the Aegean Sea alone. Every morning at sunrise, fishermen emerge from the seas with their bounty, ready to sell to the local markets. Rarely is fish sold or eaten that is more than one day old. Fish in Greece is truly the freshest you will ever find. The recipes in this chapter celebrate the flavors and the freshness of the Greek seas. Many varieties of fish indigenous to the seas surrounding Greece are not found elsewhere. I have made suggestions for fish that are widely available, such as halibut, which closely resemble the fish available locally in Greece. However, please feel free to make these recipes your own and to use any fish that you enjoy and can find locally. With seafood especially, I try to minimize the distance it must travel from the water to my table.

IN THIS CHAPTER

Bakaliaros sto Fourno *(bah-kah-LEE-AH-rohs stoh FOOR-noh)*

BAKED COD WITH LEMON GARLIC PARSLEY SAUCE

Greeks eat a lot of cod. This quick, healthy recipe is a much lighter alternative to the traditional fried cod served with *skorthalia*. The light, lemony sauce infuses the dish with a subtle garlic flavor.

SERVES 4

3 tablespoons extra-virgin olive oil, divided

4 skinless cod fillets, 6 ounces each, rinsed and patted dry

1 teaspoon sea salt, plus more to taste

4 tablespoons lemon juice, divided (about 2 lemons)

2 tablespoons finely chopped fresh Italian flat-leaf parsley

1 clove garlic, minced

1 teaspoon lemon zest

¼ teaspoon freshly ground black pepper (optional)

Preheat oven to 375 degrees.

Coat the bottom of a large oven-safe baking dish with 1 tablespoon of the olive oil. Lay the cod fillets in the baking dish and season them with ½ teaspoon of the salt (⅛ teaspoon per fillet). Drizzle 2 tablespoons of the lemon juice over the fish. Bake, uncovered, until the fish is opaque and easily flaked with a fork, about 15 minutes. Be careful not to overcook the fish.

While the fish is baking, make the sauce. In a small mixing bowl, whisk together the remaining 2 tablespoons of lemon juice, parsley, garlic, and lemon zest. Slowly whisk in the remaining 2 tablespoons of olive oil and season with the remaining ½ teaspoon salt and the pepper (if using).

Serve the cod immediately on warmed dinner plates, with the sauce spooned evenly over each fillet.

Sfiritha Fetes me Domatakia kai Elies

(sfee-REE-thah FEH-tes meh doh-mah-TAH-kee-ah keh eh-LEE-ES)

BAKED GROUPER WITH TOMATOES AND BLACK OLIVES

I think this is one of the best combinations of flavors any cook can achieve. Olives, tomatoes, and a light whitefish are not only spectacular together but also a classic representation of Mediterranean ingredients, for which the Mediterranean diet was named. You will want to make this dish again and again.

SERVES 4

20 cherry tomatoes, halved

¼ cup pitted Kalamata olives, crushed

4 cloves garlic, finely minced

1 cup loosely packed chiffonade cut fresh basil, (about 1 bunch) (see tip, page 94)

¼ cup freshly squeezed lemon juice (about 2 lemons)

3 tablespoons extra-virgin olive oil

½ teaspoon sea salt, plus more to taste

¼ teaspoon freshly ground black pepper

4 grouper fillets, 6 ounces each, rinsed and patted dry

Using your hands, gently crush the tomato halves into a medium mixing bowl, making sure to catch their juice. Stir in the crushed olives, garlic, basil, lemon juice, olive oil, salt, and pepper. Set aside to marinate at room temperature for 20 minutes.

Preheat oven to 375 degrees. Put a large baking sheet in the oven to heat while you prepare the rest of the recipe.

Cut 4 equal (12 × 15-inch) pieces of aluminum foil, large enough to make individual tents. You can also use unbleached parchment paper, if desired, by following the procedure on page 159. Lay a fillet of grouper in the center of each piece of foil. Divide the tomato and olive mixture evenly among the 4 fillets, spooning it over the top of the fish. Draw the edges of the foil upward and fold them together, like a paper lunch bag, sealing the tents closed. Be sure to leave a little space for steam to collect inside the tents. Using oven mitts and a large spatula, carefully transfer the foil tents to the hot baking sheet in the oven. Bake for 20 to 25 minutes or until the fish is cooked through.

Remove the tents from the oven and carefully cut them open, being mindful of the hot escaping steam. Serve the grouper on large plates in the foil tents.

Tsipoura sto Fourno *(TSEE-poo-rah stoh FOOR-noh)*

BAKED WHOLE RED SEA BREAM

Sea bream is a lovely, mild-tasting whitefish served all over the Mediterranean. For those of us interested in sustainable fishing practices, sea bream remains plentiful throughout the world despite its popularity. With its smooth texture and subtle flavor, sea bream is one of the most delectable whitefish available today. Give it a try!

SERVES 4

4 tablespoons extra-virgin olive oil

1 large Vidalia or yellow onion, halved and
 thinly sliced

1 large carrot, peeled and sliced into thin rounds

4 whole red sea bream, 14 to 18 ounces each,
 cleaned, scaled, gutted, and patted dry, head
 and tail intact

¾ teaspoon sea salt

½ teaspoon freshly ground black pepper

½ cup dry white wine

½ cup water

1 lemon cut into 4 wedges

1 recipe *Horiatki Salata* (page 86)

Preheat oven to 375 degrees.

Coat the bottom of a large oven-safe dish with the olive oil. Evenly distribute the onion and the carrot over the bottom of the dish. Lay each fish on top of the onion and carrot. Make 4 to 5 small slits in each sea bream and season inside and out with the salt and pepper. Slowly pour the wine and the water over the fish. Bake, uncovered, for 30 minutes. Serve with lemon wedges and *Horiatki Salata*.

———————— 🇬🇷 ————————

DEBBIE'S TIP: Cooking whole fish at home tends to stink up the place, so give my mom's trick a try. Boil a small pot of water with orange rind, a few cinnamon sticks, and some fresh rosemary for 15 to 20 minutes immediately after cooking the fish. Your house will smell fresh and clean, without a trace of fishy odor.

Bakaliaros me Prassa Patates kai Spanaki

(bah-kah-LEE-AH-rohs meh PRAH-sah pah-tah-TES keh spah-NAH-kee)

PAN-ROASTED COD WITH LEEKS, POTATOES, AND SPINACH

Leeks and cod are a match made in heaven. Add in the spinach, and you have a terrific taste-bud trio. Potatoes round out this dish with their satisfying earthiness. Though packed with healthy flavors, this dish comes together quickly and is ideal for a weeknight family supper.

SERVES 4

1 tablespoon paprika

1½ teaspoons ground cumin

¼ teaspoon cayenne pepper

1¼ teaspoons sea salt, divided, plus more to taste

4 skin-on cod fillets, 6 ounces each, cleaned, scaled, and patted dry

2 large russet potatoes, scrubbed, peeled, and cut into 1-inch dice

2 tablespoons water

2 medium leeks, cleaned very well, white and a little bit of the soft green parts thinly sliced (see tip, page 29)

2 cloves garlic, minced

1 cup vegetable broth

½ pound fresh spinach, coarse stems removed, washed in several changes of cold water, drained, and chopped

3 tablespoons extra-virgin olive oil

1 large lemon, sliced into 8 wedges

Mix together the paprika, cumin, cayenne pepper, and ½ teaspoon of the salt in a small bowl. Thoroughly coat each cod fillet with the spice mixture, rubbing it in gently. Put the fish on a large plate, cover, and refrigerate for at least 3 hours or overnight.

When ready to assemble the dish, place the potatoes in a vegetable steamer with 2 inches of water beneath and steam over medium-high heat for 20 minutes or until the potatoes are soft. Remove the potatoes from the steamer and set aside.

Meanwhile, add the water, leeks, and garlic to a large sauté pan and cook over medium-low heat, stirring occasionally, until the leeks are tender and translucent, about 15 to 20 minutes. Add a little more water every so often if the pan gets too dry. Stir in the potatoes, vegetable broth, and remaining ¾ teaspoon of salt. Increase heat to medium-high and bring to a boil. Reduce heat to medium-low, and simmer, uncovered, for 5 minutes more. Add the spinach, stir to combine, and cook just until the spinach begins to wilt. Remove from heat and transfer the vegetables to a large serving dish. Tent with aluminum foil to keep warm.

Heat the olive oil in a large nonstick skillet set over medium-high heat. Cook the fish, skin side down, for 4 minutes. Turn the fillets carefully and cook for 3 minutes more, until just cooked through and golden, especially around the edges. Remove the fish from the pan and lay the fillets over the vegetables on the serving dish. Garnish with lemon wedges and serve immediately.

Pestrofa Psiti me Lemoni kai Piperi

(PEH-stroh-fah meh leh-MOH-nee keh pee-PEH-ree)

GRILLED TROUT AND ONIONS

Trout is a perfect light summer fish, and this is an excellent recipe for a hot summer afternoon barbecue with friends and family because it cooks up in a flash. For an added treat, serve with chilled Retsina, a Greek white table wine with a bit of a kick.

SERVES 4

2 teaspoons lemon zest

¼ cup lemon juice (about 2 lemons)

¾ teaspoon sea salt

½ teaspoon freshly ground black pepper

2 tablespoons finely chopped Italian parsley

¼ cup extra-virgin olive oil, plus more for grill and onions

4 skin-on ocean or rainbow trout fillets, 6 ounces each, cleaned, scaled, and patted dry

1 large yellow onion, cut into 8 large wedges

To make the marinade, whisk the lemon zest, lemon juice, salt, pepper, and parsley in a small bowl. Slowly drizzle in the ¼ cup of olive oil, whisking constantly.

Put the trout into a large Ziploc bag and add the marinade. Squeeze out as much air as possible, and seal the bag. Shake a few times to coat the fish evenly. Set the bag on a large plate and refrigerate for 1 hour. Turn the bag over after 30 minutes.

About 20 minutes before removing the fish from the refrigerator, fire up the grill and get it hot.

When the grill is ready, lightly brush the grate with a little olive oil to prevent sticking. Brush the onions with a little olive oil as well. Lay the fish and the onions on the oiled grill; the fish should be flesh side down and skin side up at first. Grill the onions until they begin to wilt and char, about 2 to 3 minutes per side. Do the same with the fish, about 2 to 3 minutes on each side. Grill a little longer if you like your fish more well done.

Remove the fish from the grill and transfer to a large serving dish. Top with the grilled onions, and serve immediately.

———————— ⚑ ————————

DEBBIE'S TIP: I prefer an old-school charcoal grill. But don't fret if you have a gas grill—it will be delicious either way.

Psari Skorthato me Rizi kai Kolokithia

(PSAH-ree skor-thah-TOH meh REE-zee keh koh-loh-KEE-thee-ah)

GARLIC-INFUSED WHITEFISH OVER SPINACH AND SQUASH

My aunt Aphrodite has always been a very healthy eater. This recipe, one of her favorites, is high in satisfying flavor and low in fat. This is a perfect example of a recipe that fits squarely into the modern Mediterranean diet.

SERVES 4

2¼ pounds butternut squash, peeled, seeded, and cut into 1-inch cubes

2 teaspoons ground cumin

1¼ teaspoons sea salt, divided

3 tablespoons extra-virgin olive oil, divided

1 cup long-grain brown rice

4 quarts plus 2 cups water, divided

5 cloves garlic, minced, divided

½ cup finely chopped parsley

1 tablespoon lemon zest (1 lemon)

2 tablespoons freshly squeezed lemon juice (1 lemon)

4 fillets whitefish, 6 ounces each (such as red snapper, halibut, or cod), cleaned and patted dry

1½ pounds fresh spinach, coarse stems removed, washed in several changes of cold water, drained, and roughly chopped

Preheat oven to 400 degrees. Line a large baking sheet with unbleached parchment paper.

Toss the butternut squash with the cumin, ½ teaspoon of the salt, and 2 tablespoons of the olive oil on the prepared baking sheet. Evenly distribute the squash in a single layer, making sure the pieces are not too close together (otherwise the squash will steam and not roast). Bake for 45 minutes, stirring once or twice, until the squash is tender and slightly caramelized. Set aside.

Meanwhile, prepare the rice. Rinse the rice very well in a fine-mesh sieve, place it in a medium saucepan, and add 2 cups of the water, 2 cloves of the garlic, and ¼ teaspoon of the salt. Bring to a boil over medium-high heat, then reduce heat to low, stir once, cover, and simmer for 45 minutes. Remove the rice from the heat, and let rest 10 minutes, keeping lid securely in place. After 10 minutes, remove lid, and fluff with a fork. Fold together the hot rice and squash in a large mixing bowl.

Preheat oven to 300 degrees. Coat the bottom of a large oven-safe baking dish with the remaining 1 tablespoon of olive oil. Place the fish in a single layer. Stir together the parsley, lemon zest, lemon juice, the remaining ½ teaspoon of salt, and the remaining 3 cloves of garlic in a small bowl. Spoon the mixture evenly over the fish, pressing it into the flesh gently. Bake, uncovered, for 20 to 25 minutes, until the fish is cooked through and flakes easily. Do not overcook.

While the fish is cooking, bring the remaining 4 quarts of water to a boil in a large pot set over medium-high heat. Blanch the spinach in the boiling water just until it wilts, less than 1 minute. Drain well.

To serve, evenly distribute the spinach among 4 large plates. Lay a fillet of fish on the bed of spinach, and scoop a generous portion of the rice and squash alongside the fish.

Kalamaria Kaftera *(kah-lah-MAH-ree-ah kahf-teh-RAH)*

SPICY CALAMARI

Calamari has a deep and rich flavor from the sea. When it is cooked slowly, as it is in this recipe, that flavor really comes through. Don't let calamari intimidate you. This recipe is surprisingly simple to prepare, and it has a wonderfully sophisticated flavor. The red chili peppers create the heat in this recipe; feel free to add more or less depending on your preference.

SERVES 4

2 tablespoons extra-virgin olive oil

2 pounds calamari, cleaned (see tip, page 50), rings cut into ½-inch rounds, tentacles left whole

1 large Vidalia or yellow onion, halved and thinly sliced

4 ripe medium tomatoes, peeled and chopped

2 cloves garlic, finely chopped

1½ cups finely chopped fresh Italian flat-leaf parsley

1½ teaspoons fresh thyme leaves

3 bay leaves

2 small, hot red chili peppers (or to taste), thinly sliced

2½ cups dry white wine

1 teaspoon tomato paste dissolved in 2 tablespoons warm water

1 teaspoon sea salt

¼ teaspoon freshly ground black pepper

Heat the olive oil in a large stockpot or Dutch oven set over medium heat. Add the calamari and onion, and stir with a wooden spoon. After 2 minutes, add the tomatoes, garlic, parsley, thyme, bay leaves, and sliced peppers. Stir to combine, and then slowly pour in the white wine, scraping up any bits stuck to the bottom or sides of the pot. Stir in the dissolved tomato paste, and stir in the salt and pepper. Increase heat to medium-high, and bring to a boil. Reduce heat to low, cover, and simmer for 55 to 60 minutes. Remove bay leaves.

Serve hot in individual bowls with some warm, crusty bread.

Fileta Lavraki Lemonatas *(fee-LEH-tah lah-VRAH-kee leh-moh-NAH-tahs)*

LEMON-BAKED SEA BASS EN PAPILLOTE

Fish *en papillote* is a fancy way to say "fish baked in a bag." It is a classic technique that produces moist, tender, and flaky fish. Healthy, low fat, and scrumptious, it is also a simple way to create a dramatic presentation with a superfast cleanup.

SERVES 4

2 large fennel bulbs, tops removed, halved, cored, and sliced very thin

4 Mediterranean sea bass (branzini) fillets, 6 ounces each, cleaned, skinned, and patted very dry

½ teaspoon sea salt

¼ teaspoon freshly ground black pepper

½ cup freshly squeezed lemon juice (3 to 4 lemons)

⅓ cup extra-virgin olive oil

1 tablespoon chopped fresh Italian flat-leaf parsley

1 large lemon cut into 8 slices

Preheat oven to 400 degrees. Heat a large baking sheet in the oven while you prepare the rest of the recipe.

Cut 4 (15-inch) squares of unbleached parchment paper. Fold each piece of parchment in half and open it up. Place an equal amount of the sliced fennel on each square of parchment close to the crease and centered between the top and bottom edges, creating a bed of fennel for the fish to lie on. Lay a piece of fish on each of the fennel beds and season the fish evenly with the salt and pepper. Whisk together the lemon juice, olive oil, and parsley, and drizzle the mixture evenly over each fillet. Top each piece of fish with 2 slices of the lemon.

Fold the top half of each piece of parchment back over the fish and begin sealing the edges tightly by making ¼-inch folds upward toward the center of the packet. Firmly twist the top and bottom inch or two of each packet to complete the seal. You want to leave room for the parchment to puff up with steam, so take care not to stretch the parchment too tight lengthwise. Using oven mitts and a large spatula, carefully transfer the parchment packets to the hot baking sheet in the oven. Bake for 14 to 17 minutes or until the fish is cooked through and the parchment has puffed up slightly.

Remove from the oven and transfer to individual serving plates. Carefully open the packets and allow steam to escape. Serve with *Tomato, Cucumber, and Red Onion Salad* (page 97) or another seasonal salad of your choice.

DEBBIE'S TIP: You can prepare this recipe with any whitefish of similar density, such as cod, tilapia, sole, haddock, halibut, hake, flounder, or grouper. Mix it up!

Lavraki Lemonati sto Fourno

(lah-VRAH-kee leh-moh-NAH-tee stoh FOOR-noh)

LEMON-BAKED WHOLE MEDITERRANEAN SEA BASS

Baking or roasting a whole fish is one of the most common ways to prepare fish in Greece. It is flavorful, dramatic, and a very healthy way to cook fish. I always ask my fishmonger to do all the heavy lifting with respect to the cleaning, scaling, and gutting of fish. That way, when I get it home, it takes me only a few minutes to get it in the oven. This mild, flaky whitefish readily soaks up flavor, which makes this recipe so tantalizing.

SERVES 4

¾ cup extra-virgin olive oil

4 whole Mediterranean sea bass, 16 to 18 ounces each, cleaned, scaled, gutted, and patted dry, head and tail intact

2 teaspoons sea salt

1 teaspoon freshly ground black pepper, plus more to taste

3 small shallots, peeled and thinly sliced

2 cloves garlic, minced

1 large bunch fresh Italian flat-leaf parsley, finely chopped (about 1 cup)

1 teaspoon fresh thyme

1 large lemon, halved lengthwise, cut into very thin half-moon slices

Preheat oven to 375 degrees. Coat the bottom of a large baking dish with ½ cup of the olive oil.

Season the fish with the salt and pepper on both sides as well as inside the cavity. Place the fish in the baking dish and evenly distribute the shallots, garlic, parsley, and thyme over the top of each fish. Cover each fish from head to tail with the sliced lemon. Distribute any remaining lemon slices around the fish. Lightly drizzle the remaining ¼ cup of olive oil over the top of the fish. Bake, uncovered, for 30 minutes. Serve immediately.

YIAYIA'S TIP: You can substitute any whole whitefish of comparable size (like sea bream) for the sea bass in this recipe. This dish traditionally is served with a small glass of ouzo.

Marinated and Grilled Halibut

Halibut is great for a weeknight dinner because it needs to marinate only a very short time to achieve maximum flavor. It has a dense texture that stands up to the grill, but it also has a delicate flavor and, when cooked properly, is quite tender and flakes beautifully.

SERVES 4

¼ cup freshly squeezed lemon juice (about 2 lemons)

¼ cup extra-virgin olive oil

3 tablespoons finely chopped fresh Italian flat-leaf parsley, divided

2 cloves garlic, finely minced

4 halibut fillets, 6 ounces each, skinned

1 teaspoon sea salt

½ teaspoon freshly ground black pepper

4 cups loosely packed mixed greens *or* baby spinach

1 recipe *Summer Peach Salsa* (page 83) *or Latholemono* (page 73)

Whisk together the lemon juice, olive oil, 2 tablespoons of the parsley, and the garlic in a medium mixing bowl. Put the halibut in a large Ziploc bag, and pour the lemon juice mixture over the fish. Seal the bag and shake to coat the halibut in the marinade. Refrigerate on a large plate for 1 hour. Flip the bag over after 30 minutes so that the halibut marinates evenly.

Preheat a very hot grill or set a grill pan over medium-high heat. Brush the grill or grill pan with a little olive oil to prevent sticking. Remove the halibut from the marinade, season with the salt and pepper on both sides, and grill for 3 to 4 minutes per side or until cooked through. The fish is done when easily flaked with a fork. Gently lift the fish off the grill or grill pan.

Divide the greens or spinach evenly among 4 plates, and top each with a piece of halibut. Spoon the *Summer Peach Salsa* or *Latholemono* over the fish, garnish with the remaining tablespoon parsley, and serve immediately.

Lavraki Marinato me Krasi kai Skortho

(lah-VRAH-kee mah-ree-NAH-toh meh krah-SEE keh SKOR-thoh)

WINE AND GARLIC–MARINATED MEDITERRANEAN SEA BASS

Lavraki, otherwise known as Mediterranean sea bass, is called *loup* in France and *spigola* or *branzino* in Italy. In my opinion, it has one of the best flavors of all fish. In America, it is often sold as a whole fish in restaurants and high-end markets. In some fine restaurants, the chef will roast it whole, and your waiter will fillet it for you right at the table. This recipe, which came from my aunt Aphrodite, is nearly foolproof.

SERVES 4

3 garlic cloves, finely chopped

1 teaspoon lemon zest

½ cup freshly squeezed lemon juice (3 to 4 lemons)

¼ cup dry white wine

2 tablespoons finely chopped fresh Italian flat-leaf parsley

1½ teaspoons dried oregano

¾ teaspoon sea salt

3 tablespoons extra-virgin olive oil

4 whole Mediterranean sea bass, 16 ounces each, cleaned, scaled, gutted, and patted dry, heads and tails removed

In a small bowl, whisk the garlic, lemon zest, lemon juice, white wine, parsley, oregano, and salt. Slowly drizzle in the olive oil, whisking constantly.

Divide the sea bass into 2 large Ziploc bags and pour half of the marinade into each bag. Squeeze out as much air as possible, and seal the bag. Shake a few times to coat the fish evenly, making sure the marinade gets into the cavity of each fish. Refrigerate the bags on large plates for at least 3 hours, up to overnight. Turn the bags a couple of times to marinate the fish evenly.

Preheat oven to 375 degrees. Put a large baking sheet in the oven to heat while you prepare the rest of the recipe.

Remove the fish from the Ziploc bags and discard the marinade. Make aluminum foil pouches for each sea bass by placing the fish in the center of a large foil square (each about 12 × 18 inches) and drawing up the sides. Leave a little room for steam in each pouch as you fold the ends together at the top, sealing the pouch completely. Using oven mitts and a large spatula, carefully transfer the foil pouches to the hot baking sheet in the oven. Bake for 25 minutes. Remove from the oven, cut open the foil, being mindful of the escaping hot steam, and serve in the foil pouches.

DEBBIE'S TIP: I like to pair this recipe with *Tomato, Cucumber, and Onion Salad* (page 97).

Bakaliaro Tiganito *(bah-kah-LEE-AH-roh tee-ghah-nee-TOH)*

CLASSIC FRIED COD

This is the original fried cod of Greece. The light batter in which the fish is dipped crisps up in the oil, creating a perfect base on which to spread a layer of *skorthalia*. Because this is such a rich dish, portions tend to be smaller, and it's served with plenty of fresh vegetables or salads on the side.

SERVES 6 TO 8

1 large egg
½ cup all-purpose flour
½ cup milk
1½ teaspoons sea salt
Olive or vegetable oil for frying
2 pounds skinless cod fillets, cut into 4- to
    6-ounce pieces, rinsed and patted dry
1 recipe *Skorthalia Made with Potatoes* (page 81)
1 large lemon, cut into wedges

Whisk together the egg, flour, milk, and salt until smooth and well combined. The batter should resemble the consistency of a thin pancake or crepe batter.

Heat ½ inch of oil over medium-high heat until the oil shimmers and a small drop of batter dropped into the pan sizzles rapidly. Working in batches, dip the cod into the batter, coat the fish in a thin layer, and let the excess batter drip off. Immediately place the battered fish in the hot oil, and fry until cooked through and golden, about 4 to 5 minutes per side. Transfer to a large plate lined with paper towels to drain. Serve immediately with the *Skorthalia Made with Potatoes* and the lemon wedges.

Bakaliaro Tiganito sto Fourno

(bah-kah-LEE-AH-roh tee-ghah-nee-TOH stoh FOOR-noh)

OVEN-"FRIED" CRISPY COD

This is a lighter baked variation on the traditional fried cod that is served along with *skorthalia* in Greece. For some reason, cod tends to get a bad rap among foodies, but I have to tell you, it is really delicious. It is a mild, dense, flaky whitefish, loaded with vitamins and essential fatty acids. As an added benefit, cod happens to be quite affordable.

SERVES 6

Olive oil for baking rack

1 cup Vegenaise (or traditional low-fat mayonnaise)

1 tablespoon water

¼ to ½ teaspoon cayenne pepper, to taste

2 teaspoons garlic powder

1 teaspoon sweet paprika

2 teaspoons dried oregano

3 cups crouton bread crumbs made from *Easy Baked Croutons* (page 273), or store bought

2 pounds skinless cod fillets, cut into 4- to 6-ounce pieces, rinsed and patted dry

1 recipe *Skorthalia Made with Potatoes* (page 81)

1 large lemon, cut into wedges

Preheat oven to 400 degrees. Line a large baking dish or roasting pan with aluminum foil. Set an oven-safe metal baking or cooling rack into the pan, and brush the rack lightly with the olive oil to prevent sticking.

Stir together the Vegenaise, water, cayenne pepper, garlic powder, paprika, and oregano in a large shallow bowl. Spread the crouton crumbs on a large plate or baking dish. Dip the fish into the Vegenaise mixture, coating both sides completely in a thin layer. Use a knife to scrape off any excess. Then dredge the fish in the crouton bread crumbs, making sure all sides are covered, pressing the crumbs lightly to ensure they stick. Lay the breaded fillets about 1 inch apart on the prepared rack. Bake for 25 minutes or until the fish is cooked through and crispy. Serve with the *Skorthalia Made with Potatoes* and the lemon wedges.

Rizi me Thalassina *(REE-zee meh thah-lah-see-NAH)*

SEAFOOD RICE

This simple, hearty rice dish resembles a rustic and less labor-intensive risotto. It's a great way to use up leftover seafood too!

SERVES 6

3 cups water

2 cups vegetable stock

½ cup extra-virgin olive oil

1 green pepper, finely chopped

1 red bell pepper, finely chopped

1 yellow bell pepper, finely chopped

2 cups Arborio rice

3 tablespoons finely chopped fresh Italian flat-leaf parsley, divided

2 tablespoons dry white wine

1 cup fresh or frozen English peas, shelled if necessary

½ teaspoon sea salt, plus more to taste

¼ teaspoon freshly ground black pepper, plus more to taste

1 cup mussels, cooked and shelled

2 cups small shrimp, uncooked

Combine the water and vegetable stock in a small saucepan. Heat over medium heat until barely simmering. Reduce heat to low, and keep warm.

Heat olive oil in a large, heavy-bottomed pot or Dutch oven set over medium-low heat. Add the bell peppers and sauté until slightly softened, about 5 minutes. Add the rice and 2 tablespoons of the parsley, stirring constantly until the rice turns an opaque white, about 2 to 3 minutes. Stir in the wine, scraping up any brown bits, then slowly add the warm water and vegetable stock. Stir to combine well. If using fresh peas, add them at this stage, along with the salt and pepper. Reduce heat to low and cover. Cook over low heat, lifting the cover and stirring frequently to prevent scorching, until the rice is nearly done, about 20 minutes. Stir in the steamed mussels, uncooked shrimp, and frozen peas (if using instead of fresh), and cover again. Simmer for another 5 minutes just to cook the shrimp, and serve immediately, garnished with the remaining 1 tablespoon of chopped parsley.

———————— 🇬🇷 ————————

YIAYIA'S TIP: This recipe is a great use for leftover mussels, but you can steam some quickly as well. Wash the mussels well, debeard them, and put them in a large saucepan with a tight-fitting lid. Add ¼ cup white wine and ¼ cup water. Turn heat to medium-high, and cover. Steam until mussels open, about 5 minutes. Discard any mussels that do not open.

Quick and Fancy Poached Whitefish

I love to serve this quick, uncomplicated recipe when I have company. It looks very dramatic and pairs amazingly well with my no-cook *Yiaourti Lemoni kai Anitho* (page 75). I really like serving the fish with its skin, but if you're not a fan, ask your fishmonger to remove it for you.

SERVES 4 TO 6

2 pounds wild-caught whitefish fillet (such as halibut or Mediterranean sea bass), skin on if desired, scales removed

¼ teaspoon sea salt

5 lemons, ends removed, sliced into ¼-inch rounds

4 sprigs fresh dill plus ¼ cup chopped fresh dill, for garnish

2 teaspoons lemon zest

2 to 3 tablespoons freshly squeezed lemon juice (1 lemon)

2 cups white wine *or* vegetable broth, plus more as needed

½ teaspoon whole black peppercorns

1 recipe *Yiaourti Lemoni kai Anitho* (page 75) (optional)

Season the fish with the salt. In a large sauté pan with a tight-fitting lid or other pan just large enough to accommodate the fillet (such as a paella pan), make a layer of lemon slices large enough for the fish to sit on. You don't need to coat the entire bottom of the pan with lemon slices—just the portion on which the fish will sit.

You may need to trim the fillet into 2 or 3 large pieces to fit the pan.

Lay the fish on top of the lemon slices, skin side down. Lay the sprigs of dill over the top of the fish. Layer the remaining lemon slices around the sides and over the top of the fish. Mix the lemon juice and zest into the wine or vegetable broth and slowly pour the mixture over the top of the fish and into the pan. The liquid should come about halfway up the sides of the fillet. Depending on the size of the pan, you may not need to use all the liquid, or you may need to add more wine or broth. Sprinkle the peppercorns into the cooking liquid.

Turn the heat to medium-high, bring to a boil, then reduce to low, cover, and simmer for about 12 to 15 minutes or until the fish is just cooked through. Be careful not to overcook!

Cut the fish into individual servings, and serve garnished with the fresh dill and with *Yiaourti Lemoni kai Anitho,* if desired.

———————— 🇬🇷 ————————

DEBBIE'S TIP: Salmon is not indigenous to Greece, but I do enjoy this recipe with wild-caught salmon from time to time, especially when I want to mix it up.

Greek sardines in the Central Market, Athens.

A TRIP TO THE MONASTERY

Just outside of the beach village of Fanari, in Porto Lagos, there is a monastery that is open to the public each day. Built on an island in the middle of a lake and surrounded by farmland, the white buildings appear as a haven to weary travelers. One afternoon, on a whim, we decided to head over there for a quick tour. During our visit, we encountered a man we affectionately refer to as the Mysterious Monk, who was visiting from a monastery called *Agios Oros* atop the famous Mount Athos, "the holy mountain." He had arrived there with other visiting monks in anticipation of the largest holy holiday of the year in the Greek Orthodox faith, the Day of the Virgin Mary, August 15th. The Mysterious Monk seemed to be expecting us, and he welcomed us with open arms. In general, monks from *Agios Oros* are not to be photographed; however, he took a liking to us and allowed us to take photos of him as long we agreed not to show his face. The experience Peter, our photographer Jon, and I shared there together with our new friend, the Mysterious Monk, was transcendent, and though we have tried, we have yet to find words that adequately express or explain what occurred that afternoon. All I can say is that we had a profound spiritual experience that will forever live in our hearts and souls.

Hortofagos
VEGETARIAN MAIN DISHES

When my vegetarian friends accompany me on trips to Greece, they are often surprised at the wealth of dining options they have. In addition to the large variety of vegetables served at the Greek table, many classic meat-based dishes are also available vegan or vegetarian year-round. During the Lenten "fasting" periods, there are even more choices. Strict observers of the Greek Orthodox faith "fast" (keep to a vegan diet) in observance of the high holy holidays for over 180 days per year. There are four major fasting periods each year in Greece, including the Great Lent, which begins seven weeks before Easter. Even those who are not strict observers will inevitably "fast" for about two weeks per year. In my opinion, this way of eating is a perfect embodiment of the ancient Greek philosophy and way of life, which is even inscribed on the Temple of Apollo at Delphi: μηδὲν ἄγαν (*mithen agan*), which means "nothing in excess."

Araka me Anginares kai Domata

(ah-rah-KAH meh ah-NGEE-nah-res keh doh-MAH-tah)

PEAS AND ARTICHOKES WITH TOMATO

This dish was a staple in my home growing up. It's simple, delightful, and healthy, and at least in our household, it was a surefire way to get us kids to eat our peas.

SERVES 4 TO 6

1 pound fresh or frozen English peas, shelled if necessary

5 medium artichokes

3 lemons

3 teaspoons sea salt, divided

½ cup extra-virgin olive oil

4 scallions, thinly sliced, white and the most of the green

3 very ripe medium tomatoes, peeled and sliced into wedges

2 tablespoons finely chopped fresh dill

½ teaspoon freshly ground black pepper

Rinse the peas in a colander and set aside.

Wash the artichokes under cold running water. With a heavy kitchen knife, trim off the stems at the base, leaving about 1 to 1½ inches. Pull off the tough lower outer leaves. Cut off the top inch of the artichoke and rub with half of 1 lemon to prevent it from turning brown. Using kitchen shears, trim the thorny tips of the leaves. Slice the artichokes in half, again rubbing with lemon to preserve the green color, and use a small spoon or a paring knife to remove the fibrous choke from the heart.

Fill a large mixing bowl with enough water to cover artichokes and stir in 2 teaspoons of the salt along with 4 to 5 tablespoons of fresh lemon juice squeezed from the remaining lemons. Put the artichoke halves in the prepared water bath and set aside.

Heat the olive oil in a large pot set over medium heat. Add the scallions and sauté for 1 to 2 minutes. Add the tomato and remaining 1 teaspoon of salt. Cook, stirring frequently, until the tomatoes begin to break down, about 3 minutes. Add the peas and stir to combine. Drain and rinse artichokes and put them on top of the peas, stems facing up. Sprinkle the dill on top and pour in 1 cup of warm water. Cook for 35 minutes over medium heat or until the liquid has evaporated. Stir in black pepper, taste, and adjust seasoning, if necessary.

VARIATION: Instead of tomatoes, add the juice of 2 more lemons as well as the zest of 1 lemon plus 1 extra cup of water. Cook as directed.

Araka me Anginares kai Domata (opposite)

Kritharaki me Domata kai Feta (see next page)

Kritharaki me Domata kai Feta

(kree-thah-RAH-kee meh doh-MAH-tah keh FEH-tah)

ORZO WITH TOMATOES AND FETA

Orzo, tomatoes, and feta are classic Greek kitchen staples that combine to create a quick, luscious pasta dish. Serve with crusty bread and a fresh salad for a hearty and delicious meal that is ready in no time.

SERVES 4

4 tablespoons extra-virgin olive oil, divided

1 medium yellow or red onion, finely chopped

2 cloves garlic, finely chopped

½ teaspoon sea salt, plus more to taste

¼ teaspoon freshly ground pepper

¼ teaspoon crushed red pepper flakes (optional)

1 recipe *Mama's Domata Saltsa* (page 74)

4 quarts water

1 pound dried orzo

½ cup chiffonade-cut fresh basil (see tip, page 94)

¼ to ½ cup brine-packed Greek feta, crumbled small

Heat 2 tablespoons of the olive oil in a large saucepan over medium heat. Add the onion and sauté until translucent, 5 to 6 minutes, stirring frequently. Stir in the garlic, salt, pepper, and crushed red pepper flakes (if using) and cook for 1 minute more. Add the stewed tomatoes and simmer for 10 minutes, covered, over very low heat. Taste and adjust seasonings, if necessary. Ladle out 1 cup of the sauce, and reserve.

Bring the 4 quarts of water, liberally salted, to a boil. Add the orzo and cook for about 7 minutes, leaving it slightly undercooked. Ladle 1 cup of the pasta cooking water into the reserved tomato sauce. Drain the orzo well and add it to the tomato sauce. Stir to combine and cook over low heat for 1 to 2 minutes, until the orzo is al dente and well coated in the sauce. If the orzo seems dry, add some of the reserved sauce, a couple of tablespoons at a time, to taste.

Remove from heat and stir in the basil, the remaining 2 tablespoons of olive oil, and the feta. Serve immediately, passing any remaining tomato sauce at the table.

DEBBIE'S TIP: To make this dish vegan, simply omit the feta cheese. Without feta, this dish is a light accompaniment or bed for many of the heartier dishes throughout the book.

Makaronia me Yiaourti (mah-kah-ROH-nee-ah meh yah-OOR-tee)

SPAGHETTI WITH GREEK YOGURT

Pasta with a yogurt sauce is a classic combination in Greece and Turkey. The yogurt provides the comforting unctuousness of a heavy cream sauce, reminiscent of the Italian classic spaghetti alla carbonara, but instead of being weighed down with calories and fat, it is far lighter and healthier. I prefer to use whole wheat spaghetti for a heartier, more nutritious meal.

SERVES 4 TO 6

½ cup extra-virgin olive oil

2 medium yellow onions, finely chopped

2 cloves garlic, finely chopped

4 quarts water

1 pound whole wheat or other spaghetti

2 cups Greek yogurt, at room temperature

1 cup freshly grated kefalotiri *or* Parmesan cheese

¼ teaspoon sea salt, plus more to taste

½ teaspoon freshly ground black pepper, plus more to taste

¼ cup chopped fresh Italian flat-leaf parsley, for garnish

Heat the olive oil in a large skillet or sauté pan set over medium-low heat. Add the onion and cook, stirring frequently, until it is translucent, about 8 to 10 minutes. Stir in the garlic and cook for 1 minute more. Remove from heat and set aside to cool slightly.

Add the water to a large pot and bring to a boil over high heat. When the water starts to boil, liberally salt it (see tip). Add the spaghetti and cook for 1 minute less than the package directions, until al dente. While the pasta is cooking, mix together the yogurt, cheese, salt, and pepper in a medium mixing bowl, making sure there are no lumps.

Drain the pasta, reserving 1 cup of the starchy cooking water. Return the hot pasta to its pot, and add the olive oil–onion mixture, tossing to combine well and coat the spaghetti. Quickly add the yogurt mixture, making sure the spaghetti is coated. Very slowly pour in the reserved cooking water, a little at a time, until the desired consistency is reached. You probably will not need all the water.

Transfer to individual serving bowls or onto a large serving platter. Garnish with the parsley and serve immediately.

YIAYIA'S TIP: Pasta should be cooked in water that tastes like the sea. Adding salt to the water seasons the pasta as it cooks, which means that your finished dish will have more complex flavor, and you may not need as much salt in the sauce or the finished dish. Cook pasta in plenty of water, seasoned with 1 to 2 tablespoons of salt.

Gigantes *(GHEE-ghan-des)*

GREEK GIANT WHITE BEANS

Gigantes means "giants," and that is exactly what these beans are. You can find them in Greek specialty stores or online (see page 33). If you cannot find Greek *gigantes,* you can substitute large butter beans; however, I do recommend using the authentic Greek *gigantes* for this recipe whenever possible. They are so good!

Gigantes are served in every Greek household, and they were always my favorite bean dish. When I was a kid, I used to think they tasted just like SpaghettiOs, and that's exactly how my mom tricked me into eating them! Mom rarely served anything that wasn't homemade, so the idea of eating anything from a can was like heaven to me. Of course, I now think home-made *gigantes* are so much better than anything that comes from a can. You can eat them hot or cold. Either way, they are the best-tasting faux SpaghettiOs I've ever eaten.

SERVES 6 TO 8

1 pound dried *gigantes* beans, picked over, rinsed, and soaked overnight
¼ cup extra-virgin olive oil
1 large Vidalia or other sweet onion, finely chopped
2 cloves garlic, finely chopped
3 tablespoons finely chopped fresh Italian flat-leaf parsley, divided
1 recipe *Mama's Domata Saltsa* (page 74)
1½ teaspoons sea salt
Freshly ground pepper, to taste

Drain and rinse the soaked beans, and put them in a large pot with enough water to cover generously, by at least 3 inches. Bring to a boil over medium-high heat, reduce heat to low, and cover. Simmer for about 1 hour, until tender, stirring occasionally. Add more water, if necessary, to keep the beans covered.

When the beans are tender, drain them in a large colander, rinse well with cold water, and carefully remove the shells. This process takes patience and time. Squeeze each bean from the bottom to pop it out of its shell without crushing or breaking it. Set the shelled beans aside.

Preheat oven to 350 degrees. Lightly oil a large oven-safe baking dish and set aside.

Heat the olive oil over medium heat in a sauté pan and add the chopped onion. Cook, stirring frequently, until the onion has slightly browned, about 7 or 8 minutes. Add the garlic and cook for 1 minute more. Stir the onion mixture, salt, pepper, and 2 tablespoons of the chopped parsley into the stewed tomatoes.

Put the beans in the prepared baking dish, and pour the tomato sauce over, submerging them completely. Bake, uncovered, on the center oven rack for 1 hour, until hot and bubbly. Let cool for 15 minutes.

Garnish with remaining 1 tablespoon of parsley. Serve hot or cold.

Papoutsakia Lathera *(pah-poo-TSAH-kee-ah lah-theh-RAH)*

STUFFED EGGPLANT

The literal translation of *papoutsakia* is "little shoes." This dish got its name from the resemblance of the eggplant's cooked exterior to black leather shoes. Don't let the name fool you. This eggplant dish is so mouthwatering that you'll be left licking your lips.

SERVES 4 TO 6

4 teaspoons sea salt, divided

4 tablespoons extra-virgin olive oil, divided

3 to 3½ pounds eggplant (3 medium eggplant)

2 large yellow onions, chopped

1 pound large ripe tomatoes, peeled, seeded, and chopped

3 cloves garlic, finely chopped

¼ cup finely chopped fresh Italian flat-leaf parsley

¼ cup finely chopped fresh mint

1 teaspoon freshly ground black pepper

1 5.5-ounce can low-sodium V8 juice

Preheat oven to 350 degrees.

Fill a large mixing bowl with water and stir in 2 teaspoons of the salt. Using 2 tablespoons of the olive oil, oil a baking dish large enough to hold the eggplant halves in 1 layer.

Partially peel the eggplant lengthwise in 1-inch strips all the way around. Slice each eggplant in half lengthwise down the middle. With a small teaspoon or a grapefruit spoon, hollow out the inside of all the eggplant, leaving about ⅛ inch of pulp still attached to the skin. Reserve the remaining pulp. Set the empty eggplant shells in the prepared baking dish, turning them slightly to coat their outsides with some of the oil from the dish. Place the baking dish in the oven, and bake for 15 minutes to soften the eggplant shells. Remove from oven, and set aside to cool.

Submerge the eggplant pulp in the bowl of salted water for 2 to 3 minutes. Remove the pulp from the water, and place in a colander. Set a plate on top of the eggplant, and put a weight (such as a large can of tomatoes) on top of the plate to help squeeze out more water. Set the colander in the sink and let the eggplant drain for 15 to 20 minutes. Rinse the eggplant very well under cold running water for 2 to 3 minutes. Gently squeeze the excess water from the eggplant, dice into ¼-inch cubes, and set aside.

Coat the inside of a large sauté pan with the remaining 2 tablespoons of olive oil. Set over medium heat and add the onion and tomato. Sauté for about 12 to 14 minutes, stirring occasionally, until the onion is translucent and the tomato has begun to make a broth. Add the garlic and cook for 2 more minutes. Then add the parsley, mint, diced eggplant pulp, remaining 2 teaspoons of salt, and pepper. Stir to combine well and cook for 7 to 8 minutes, stirring occasionally, until the eggplant softens. Remove from heat.

Using a large spoon, carefully fill each half eggplant shell with the cooked eggplant mixture. Pour the V8 juice over the top of the stuffed eggplant. Bake, uncovered, for 50 to 55 minutes. For a crispier dish, broil for the last 1 to 2 minutes, watching very closely to make sure the tops do not burn. Serve immediately.

YIAYIA'S TIP: To make the dish extra-rich and comforting, add a layer of *Béchamel Sauce* (page 71) on top. Spoon the sauce over the top during the last 15 minutes of cooking, allowing it to brown slightly but taking care not to allow it to burn. Alternatively, you can top the stuffed eggplant with 1 cup of crumbled feta cheese. Sprinkle the feta on top for the last 5 minutes of baking.

Gemista *(gheh-mee-STAH)*

STUFFED PEPPERS AND TOMATOES

Growing up, I loved coming home after Greek school and walking through the door to the smell of my mom's *gemista*. I can still recognize that smell anywhere. It's very nostalgic for me and always makes my mouth water! My vegan version of this classic dish uses brown rice instead of white rice and mushrooms and zucchini as a healthy, low-fat substitute for the traditional beef. Brown rice is more nutritious, tends to hold up better, and adds a subtle, nutty flavor.

SERVES 6

½ cup plus 1 tablespoon extra-virgin olive oil, divided, plus more for baking dish

1 medium yellow onion, finely chopped

1 cup long-grain brown rice

2¼ cups low-sodium vegetable broth

2¼ teaspoons sea salt, divided

4 large bell peppers of various colors (green, red, yellow, or orange)

2 large tomatoes

2 tablespoons tomato paste diluted in 1 cup water

¾ pound sliced cremini *or* white button mushrooms

½ pound zucchini, ends trimmed, sliced into ¼-inch rounds

1 teaspoon freshly ground black pepper

¼ cup finely chopped fresh Italian flat-leaf parsley

1½ tablespoons finely chopped fresh mint

¼ cup water, plus more as needed

Heat 2 tablespoons of the olive oil in a medium saucepan set over medium heat. Add the onion and sauté until translucent but not browned, about 5 minutes, stirring frequently. Add the brown rice and cook, stirring constantly, until lightly toasted, about 2 minutes. Slowly stir in the vegetable broth and ¼ teaspoon of the salt, increase heat to medium-high, and bring to a boil. Reduce heat, cover, and simmer until all the liquid has been absorbed, about 45 minutes. Remove from heat and let stand, covered, for about 10 minutes. Then remove lid, fluff the rice with a fork, and set aside.

Meanwhile, lightly oil a deep casserole dish large enough to hold all the peppers and tomatoes snugly so that they remain upright during baking.

Slice off and reserve the top stem ends of the bell peppers. Hollow out the peppers, removing the seeds and white pith with a small spoon or a grapefruit spoon and discarding. Slice off and reserve the top stem ends of the tomatoes. Gently squeeze the tomatoes to remove most of the seeds, then scoop the pulp into a small bowl, leaving a thin layer of tomato (about ¼ inch) next to the skin. Stir the diluted tomato paste into the tomato pulp and set aside. Transfer the hollowed-out tomatoes and peppers to the prepared casserole dish. Set aside.

(recipe continues)

Preheat oven to 350 degrees.

Heat 3 tablespoons of the olive oil in a large stockpot or Dutch oven over medium-high heat. Add the mushrooms and sauté until the edges start to brown and they release their liquid, about 4 to 6 minutes. Add the zucchini slices and sauté until wilted and cooked through, 2 to 3 minutes more. Season with the remaining 2 teaspoons of salt and the pepper. Stir in the reserved tomato mixture and the cooked onion and rice. Bring to a boil, reduce heat to low, and simmer for 1 to 2 minutes, just to let the flavors come together. At this point, the mixture should be moist but not soupy. If it is too loose, simmer it a little longer to evaporate a bit more of the liquid, being careful not to overcook the rice. Turn off the heat and stir in the parsley and the mint. Taste and adjust seasonings, if necessary.

Generously stuff the tomatoes and bell peppers with the rice mixture. Replace the pepper and tomato tops. The stuffing will peek out a bit. Drizzle with the remaining ¼ cup of olive oil and carefully pour the water into the bottom of the casserole. Bake, adding a little more water if necessary, for 1 to 1¼ hours or until the vegetables are tender and the tops are brown. The tomatoes and peppers should be soft enough to pierce easily with a fork. Serve immediately.

———————— ≡ ————————

DEBBIE'S TIP: The classic version of this dish is made with lean ground beef. My vegan version makes a savory, light supper with no saturated fat. If you do want to try it the traditional way, replace the mushrooms and zucchini with 1 pound of lean ground beef or turkey.

Briam (bree-AHM)

BAKED EGGPLANT, ZUCCHINI, AND POTATOES

Briam, a classic Greek dish, is known to northern Greeks by its Turkish name, *tourli*. Northern Greece has adopted many Turkish words into its regional vocabulary due to its proximity to the Turkish border. In fact, I grew up not realizing that I spoke quite a bit of Turkish!

SERVES 6 TO 8

5 medium tomatoes, peeled
2 large russet potatoes, peeled
3 small eggplant
5 medium zucchini
½ cup finely chopped Vidalia or yellow onion
2 tablespoons finely chopped red bell pepper (about ½ pepper)
3 to 4 cloves garlic, finely chopped (about 1 tablespoon)
2 teaspoons sea salt
2 teaspoons freshly ground black pepper
1 teaspoon dried oregano
½ to ¾ cup extra-virgin olive oil, to taste
2 tablespoons finely chopped fresh Italian flat-leaf parsley
½ cup brine-packed Greek feta, crumbled, for garnish (optional)

Preheat oven to 300 degrees. Oil a 9 × 13-inch baking dish.

Cut the tomatoes, potatoes, eggplant, and zucchini into ¼-inch-thick rounds. Mix the onion, bell pepper, and garlic together in a small mixing bowl. Mix the salt, pepper, and oregano together in another small bowl.

Cover the bottom of the prepared baking dish with half of the tomato slices. Evenly sprinkle one-third of the spice mixture over the tomato slices. Then evenly distribute half of the onion, bell pepper, and garlic mixture over the tomato slices.

Lay alternating lengthwise rows of the sliced potatoes, eggplant, and zucchini in the baking dish, forming a tight, single layer. Sprinkle one-third of the spice mixture over the top of the vegetables. Follow again with the remaining onion, bell pepper, and garlic mixture. Add the remaining sliced tomatoes to cover. Sprinkle the top layer of tomatoes with the remaining spice mixture and the parsley. Drizzle the olive oil evenly over the top of the casserole.

Bake, uncovered, for 1½ hours, until the vegetables are very tender and the top begins to brown. Check after 45 minutes to see if the vegetables are getting too dry. If so, add ½ cup of warm water to moisten.

Remove from oven, and let cool for 10 minutes. Cut into pieces, and serve. Sprinkle 1 tablespoon or so of the feta cheese (if using) over the top of each piece before serving.

Strapatsatha (strah-pah-TSAH-thah)

EGGS WITH TOMATO

This seems like a breakfast dish, but it traditionally is served for a quick, easy, and delicious lunch or light supper. *Strapatsatha* was my dad's favorite meal. He'd ask my mom to prepare it for dinner at least once a week.

SERVES 4 TO 6

3 tablespoons extra-virgin olive oil

5 very ripe medium tomatoes, peeled, seeded, and cut into 6 wedges each

½ teaspoon sea salt, divided

5 large eggs

¼ teaspoon freshly ground black pepper

Heat the olive oil in a medium nonstick sauté pan over medium-low heat. Add the tomatoes and ¼ teaspoon of the salt and cook, stirring frequently, until the tomatoes break down and their liquid has evaporatcd, about 15 to 20 minutes.

Beat the eggs together with the remaining salt and the pepper. Reduce heat to a low simmer and stir the eggs into the tomatoes with a wooden spoon. Cook, stirring and fluffing the eggs, for 4 to 6 minutes, or until they have just set but are still a little soft. Do not overcook the eggs—they will continue to cook even when they are no longer in the pan.

Remove the pan from heat, and transfer to a large serving dish. Spoon any tomato sauce remaining in the pan over the eggs. Serve immediately.

Revithia *(reh-VEE-thee-ah)*

GREEK-STYLE LEMON CHICKPEAS

This hearty and delicious vegan main dish is always a hit, whether I'm having a big party or a small supper with friends. It goes great with *Pilafi* (page 230) made with vegetable broth and *Oven-Roasted Broccoli with Lemon* (page 234).

SERVES 4 TO 6

FOR THE CHICKPEAS

1 cup dried chickpeas (garbanzo beans), soaked for 8 hours or overnight

2 cloves garlic, smashed and peeled

2 bay leaves

½ teaspoon sea salt

FOR THE FINISHED DISH

¼ cup extra-virgin olive oil, plus more to taste

1½ cups red onion, diced (about ½ large red onion)

2 cloves garlic, minced

1 teaspoon dried oregano

¼ teaspoon sea salt, plus more to taste

¼ teaspoon freshly ground black pepper

¼ cup water

2 tablespoons chopped fresh Italian flat-leaf parsley

2 teaspoons lemon zest

¼ cup freshly squeezed lemon juice (about 2 lemons)

½ cup *Tahini Sauce* (page 82), plus more to taste

Drain and rinse the soaked beans, transfer them to a large pot, and cover with fresh water by 1 inch. Bring to a boil over medium-high heat and cook for 2 minutes, skimming off any foam that rises to the surface. Reduce heat to medium-low, add the garlic and bay leaves, and simmer, covered with a tilted lid, for 30 minutes. Stir in the salt, replace the tilted lid, and continue cooking for another 20 to 30 minutes, until the beans are very tender. Remove from heat and let cool slightly. Drain, discard garlic and bay leaves, and set aside.

Heat the olive oil in a large pot or Dutch oven set over medium heat. Add the onion and cook until translucent, about 5 minutes, stirring frequently. Add the garlic, oregano, salt, and pepper, and cook for 1 minute more. Stir in the water, scraping up any brown bits stuck to the bottom or sides of the pot. Stir in the cooked chickpeas and the parsley, and simmer for a couple of minutes, stirring frequently, to warm everything through. Remove from heat, and add the lemon zest and lemon juice. Stir in the *Tahini Sauce*, a little at a time, until desired consistency is reached. Taste and adjust seasonings, if necessary. Serve immediately.

DEBBIE'S TIP: You can easily make this recipe with canned beans. Use 2 (15-ounce) cans garbanzo beans.

THE BUTCHERS OF FANARI

In the small beach village of Fanari, where my family has a home, there is but one local butcher shop owned and run by the Gkanios family, which is called simply Gka nios Butcher Shop. As is often the story in Greece, the Gkanios family has owned their butcher shop in Fanari for over forty-three years. Kostas Gkanios runs the shop with his wife Veta and daughter Nena. Kostas's father, Stavros, actually started the business back in

1970 in a different, smaller location, where the shop remained for thirty-eight years. Back when Stavros first opened his doors, he did not have any of the modern mixing, vacuum, or sausage stuffing machines they have today. He did everything by hand, and they continued to do everything by hand until just five years ago, when they moved a couple of doors down to a larger space and modernized the operation. His daughter Nena is truly a woman of the modern age. She felt that the local residents of Fanari needed to be bilingual. Thus, she opened a small English school behind the butcher shop to teach the local residents, especially children, English. Using all the latest technological advances in linguistics, she holds classes from 3 P.M. to 9 P.M. five days per week.

Kreata kai Kotopoulo
MEAT AND POULTRY MAIN DISHES

Even though some of the most famous Greek dishes are meat based, in the traditional Greek diet, meat tends to play a secondary role to fresh vegetables, due to their overwhelming abundance. Still, if there were a national meat of Greece, it would be lamb. There are so many ways to prepare lamb, but I have tried to provide a few of my favorite classics in this chapter. Beef, pork, and poultry also find their way onto the Greek table at mealtime, and all frequently are seasoned with the traditional flavors of lemon, oregano, parsley, and garlic. Usually these rich, savory dishes serve many people family style—just a small serving per person should do the trick.

Arni Frikase me Avgolemono *(ahr-NEE free-kah-SEH ah-VGHO-leh-moh-noh)*

LAMB FRICASSEE WITH AVGOLEMONO

You really cannot get any more traditional than this dish! Lamb cooked in this manner is incredibly tender and flavorful. In America, it is not very common to cook lettuce, but in Greece, several traditional dishes feature cooked greens typically reserved for raw salads. Although it may seem out of the ordinary, the combination of cooked romaine lettuce with the tender lamb makes this dish a real standout.

SERVES 4 TO 5

2½ pounds boneless leg of lamb, trimmed and cut into 3-inch chunks

3 tablespoons extra-virgin olive oil

10 scallions, thinly sliced, white and green parts separated

1 cup warm water, plus more as needed

4 teaspoons sea salt, divided, plus more to taste

2 medium heads romaine lettuce, shredded

1 tablespoon finely chopped fresh dill

1½ teaspoons freshly ground black pepper

1 recipe *Avgolemono* (page 70), made with the broth from the lamb

Rinse the lamb, and pat dry with paper towels. Heat the olive oil in a large stockpot or Dutch oven set over medium heat. Add the lamb and brown on all sides, about 4 to 5 minutes on each side. Add the white parts of the scallions and cook until translucent, 2 to 3 minutes, stirring frequently. Add 1 cup of warm water and 2 teaspoons of the salt, increase heat to medium-high, and bring to a boil. Reduce heat to medium-low and simmer, uncovered and stirring occasionally to prevent scorching, for 15 to 20 minutes or until the lamb is tender and cooked through.

Add the romaine lettuce, dill, remaining 2 teaspoons of salt, and pepper. Cover and cook over low heat for 15 minutes. Gently stir the meat every 5 minutes or so and add a bit more water if needed. (Do not add water at the same time you add the lettuce, as lettuce contains quite a bit of water that will be released as soon as it starts to cook.) After 15 minutes, remove from heat.

Make the *Avgolemono* using the broth from the lamb as the broth for the sauce. Slowly add the sauce back into the pot with the lamb. Cover and shake the pot to coat the lamb evenly and distribute the sauce. Do not stir.

Garnish with the reserved green parts of the scallions, and serve.

Dolmathes me Lahano Avgolemono

(DOHL-mah-thes meh LAH-hah-noh ah-VGHO-leh-moh-noh)

STUFFED CABBAGE WITH AVGOLEMONO

Whenever I cook this meal, I am reminded of my dad. This dish, one of the most traditional in Greece, was a favorite of his, and I have always loved it too. It is served primarily in the winter, because, according to the Greek farmers, good cabbage becomes available only after the first frost. Although they are a bit labor-intensive, these tasty stuffed cabbage rolls will warm the belly and the soul, making every bite worth all the effort!

SERVES 6 TO 8

1 large head green cabbage

1 large yellow onion, finely grated

1 pound lean ground beef or turkey

½ cup long-grain white rice, rinsed well

1 large egg

¼ cup finely chopped fresh parsley

4 tablespoons extra-virgin olive oil, divided

2 teaspoons ground cumin (optional)

1 tablespoon sea salt

1½ teaspoons freshly ground black pepper, plus more to garnish

1 recipe *Avgolemono* (page 70), made with the broth from the cabbage

Carefully cut out the stem of the cabbage, keeping the leaves intact. Lower the cabbage, cut (stem) end down, into a large pot of water, ensuring that there is enough water to keep cabbage fully submerged. Cover and bring to a boil over medium-high heat.

As soon as the water begins to boil and the cabbage leaves begin to open, use the back sides of 2 large spoons pressed together to grip each cabbage leaf in order to slowly remove each leaf without tearing it. Collect the separated cabbage leaves in a large pan or dish. Continue this process until you have removed all the cabbage leaves. When finished, reserve the cabbage cooking water from the pot to make the sauce.

Combine the grated onion, ground beef or turkey, rice, egg, parsley, 2 tablespoons of olive oil, cumin (if using), salt, and pepper in a large mixing bowl and mix well with impeccably clean hands. Set aside.

As shown on the opposite page, slice 1 inch or so off the bottom of each cabbage leaf (where it connected to the stem) and discard. Place 1 heaping tablespoon of the meat mixture in the center of a cabbage leaf. Fold in each side, roll it up like a burrito, and set aside on a clean plate or in a large pan. Continue with the remaining leaves until all filling is used up.

(recipe continues)

Line the bottom of a large, deep stockpot with the remainder of the cabbage leaves. Put all of the cabbage rolls (*dolmathes*) in the pot, neatly lining them up along the bottom. When the bottom layer is full, stack the rolls in a second layer. Drizzle the remaining 2 tablespoons olive oil over the top, then pour the reserved cabbage broth over the top until the cabbage rolls are nearly covered but not fully submerged. Gently lay a clean heatproof plate on top of the rolls inside the pot. (The plate should fit inside but be large enough to cover all the rolls.) Cover and cook over medium heat for 60 minutes or until the rice and beef are fully cooked. Poke with a fork to check doneness. Remove from heat, and carefully remove the plate covering the cabbage rolls.

Make the *Avgolemono* using the broth from the cabbage cooking pot as the broth for the sauce. Pour the sauce over the top of the cabbage rolls, cover, and shake gently from side to side to coat the rolls evenly and distribute the sauce.

Serve immediately, garnished with a few grinds of fresh pepper.

———————— 🇬🇷 ————————

DEBBIE'S TIP: When I was a kid, I ate so much *avgolemono,* I thought I'd start clucking! For a refreshing change, omit the sauce. Add 2 tablespoons tomato paste to the beef and rice mixture. Seed and dice 3 large tomatoes, and scatter over the *dolmathes* before cooking.

YIAYIA'S TIP: As you become more proficient at tightly rolling perfect *dolmathes*, you can stop using the dinner plate to cover them in the pot. The plate simply ensures that the rolls do not open as they cook.

Lemonati Kota sta Karvouna (leh-moh-NAH-tee KOH-tah stah KAR-voo-nah)

LEMONY GRILLED CHICKEN

I have found that simple food with great flavor is often the most satisfying, healthy, and easy to prepare. This fast and fantastic chicken recipe is packed with flavor and can be doubled or tripled easily for a big crowd. Serve this chicken with *Summer Peach Salsa* for a great summer lunch or light dinner. You can make the salsa and start to marinate the chicken right before you leave for work in the morning. Then, when you come home, just toss the chicken on the grill, and you can have a healthy dinner on the table in about 20 minutes.

SERVES 4

¼ cup freshly squeezed lemon juice (about 2 lemons)

¼ cup extra-virgin olive oil

2 teaspoons dried oregano

5 scallions, soft green parts reserved, thinly sliced

4 skinless, boneless chicken breasts

1 teaspoon sea salt, plus more to taste

½ teaspoon freshly ground black pepper

4 cups loosely packed mixed greens or baby spinach

1 recipe *Summer Peach Salsa* (page 83) or *Latholemono* (page 73)

In a medium mixing bowl, whisk together the lemon juice, olive oil, oregano, and the white parts of the scallions. Set aside.

Rinse the chicken under cold water, pat dry with paper towels, and season on both sides with the salt and pepper. Put the chicken into a large Ziploc bag and pour in the lemon juice mixture. Squeeze out as much air as possible, seal the bag, and shake to coat chicken in the marinade. Refrigerate on a large plate for at least 1 hour or up to overnight. Flip the bag over at least once so that the chicken marinates evenly.

Prepare a very hot grill or set a grill pan over medium-high heat. Brush the grill or grill pan with a little olive oil to prevent sticking. Remove the chicken from the marinade and grill for 4 to 6 minutes per side or until cooked through. Remove from the grill and let the chicken rest for about 10 minutes before serving.

To serve, evenly distribute the greens among 4 plates. Slice the chicken breasts into 1-inch diagonal slices and fan the slices over the greens. Spoon the *Summer Peach Salsa* or *Latholemono* over the top of the chicken. Garnish with the reserved green parts of the scallions. This chicken is also delicious served with *Tzatziki* (page 76).

Kolokithakia Gemista me Kima

(koh-loh-kee-THAH-kee-ah gheh-mee-STAH meh kee-MAH)

STUFFED ZUCCHINI

Many vegetables in Greece are stuffed. Tomatoes, peppers, eggplant, cabbage leaves, and grape leaves are all examples of vegetables that are often filled with a savory meat or vegetable medley. Zucchini is certainly no exception! In this recipe, it is stuffed with meat and rice, and we reserve the pulp to make *Kolokithopites* (page 56), which are savory zucchini fritters. You can serve these morsels of deliciousness with or without *Avgolemono*. They are great both ways.

SERVES 4 TO 6

3 pounds medium zucchini, washed
    and stemmed
¾ cup extra-virgin olive oil , divided
1 medium yellow onion, finely chopped
1 pound very lean ground beef
3 tablespoons finely chopped fresh Italian
    flat-leaf parsley
1 tablespoon finely chopped fresh mint
2½ teaspoons sea salt
1½ teaspoons freshly ground black pepper
3 cups warm water, divided
½ cup long-grain white rice
½ cup grated kefalotiri *or* Parmesan cheese
2 large eggs, separated, yolks reserved for
    Avgolemono
1 recipe *Avgolemono* (page 70), made with
    cooking liquid from stuffed zucchini
    (optional)

Cut the zucchini in half down the center into half cylinders. With a small teaspoon or a grapefruit spoon, hollow out the zucchini skins by scooping out all the pulp, leaving about ⅛ inch of zucchini intact next to the skin. Leave the bottoms intact so that you are left with a "zucchini cup" in which to stuff the filling. Take care not to crack or puncture the skins. Set the zucchini cups aside while you make the filing. Cover and reserve the zucchini pulp in the refrigerator to make *Kolokithopites*.

Heat ½ cup of the olive oil in a large pot set over medium heat. Add the onion and cook until lightly browned, 8 to 10 minutes. Add the beef and cook until no longer pink and lightly browned, about 8 to 10 minutes, breaking up any large chunks with a spoon. Stir in the parsley, mint, salt, and pepper. Add ½ cup of the warm water. Increase heat to medium-high, bring to a boil, reduce heat to low, and simmer, uncovered, for 10 minutes. Add 1½ cups more of the warm water. Increase heat to medium-high, bring to a boil again, and add the rice. Stir once, reduce heat, cover, and simmer for 20 minutes. Remove from heat, stir in the cheese, and let cool, uncovered, for 10 minutes.

Vigorously beat the 2 egg whites until fluffy, then gently fold them into the meat mixture. Fill the zucchini cups with the meat mixture. Neatly arrange the stuffed zucchini horizontally in a wide, deep pot or Dutch oven, stacking multiple layers if necessary. Evenly pour the remaining ¼ cup of olive oil and 1 cup of warm water over the zucchini, and set the pot over medium-high heat. Bring to a boil, immediately reduce heat to low, cover, and simmer for 20 minutes. Remove from heat and carefully remove 1 cup of cooking liquid from the pot if making the *Avgolemono*.

Make the *Avgolemono*, if desired, using the reserved cooking liquid. Pour the finished sauce over the stuffed zucchini, cover, and shake gently from side to side to coat the zucchini evenly and distribute the sauce.

Serve immediately.

Souvlaki Arni (*soo-VLAH-kee ahr-NEE*)

LAMB SOUVLAKI

Souvlaki is the all-time classic! It is the Greek equivalent of the American hot dogs and hamburgers. To make this recipe so much easier, ask your butcher to carve the leg of lamb into 1½-inch cubes. Be sure to save the bone to make *Greek Easter Soup* (page 132), which is delicious. This recipe is designed as a main course, but it can also be a fun appetizer for a party. In my opinion, *Souvlaki* is best made on an outdoor charcoal grill. You can make these in the oven, but the grill is most authentic and tasty.

SERVES 6 TO 8

1 leg of lamb (bone-in weight about
   6 to 7½ pounds), meat cut into 1½-inch
   cubes, bone reserved for another use
1 tablespoon sea salt
2 teaspoons freshly ground pepper
15 shish kebab sticks, soaked in water at least
   20 minutes (if wooden) to prevent burning
½ cup extra-virgin olive oil
6 tablespoons freshly squeezed lemon juice
   (about 2 lemons)
1 tablespoon dried oregano

Heat an outdoor grill (charcoal is best) for 30 minutes, getting the flame to about medium heat.

Thoroughly wash the lamb. Pat dry with paper towels, and season with the salt and pepper. Let the seasoned lamb rest for 15 minutes at room temperature before proceeding.

Meanwhile, mix the olive oil, lemon juice, and oregano together in a mixing bowl. Fire up the grill and get it hot.

Assemble the *souvlaki*: Spear about 5 pieces of lamb onto each soaked shish kebab stick. Put the lamb on the grill. With a pastry brush, baste each kebab with the lemon juice mixture, being sure to coat each side of the meat. Continue down the line, then start over again at the beginning, until you have used up all the lemon juice mixture. Cook the lamb on the grill for 10 minutes total, turning every couple of minutes until browned on all sides. Remove from heat when done and serve.

VARIATION: This same recipe can be made with pork, chicken, or beef.

Moussaka *(moo-sah-KAH)*

Sunday is a big day for food in Greek households. It certainly was in mine. Typically it is a day when extended family and friends gather together to cook and enjoy a big afternoon meal. *Moussaka* was quite often the star of these Sunday afternoon gatherings. It takes some time to put together, but trust me, you will love the end result! However, keep in mind that the ancient inscription on the Temple of Apollo at Delphi, which reads "Nothing in excess," definitely applies here.

SERVES 10 TO 12

2 large eggplant (about 1½ pounds each), sliced
    into ¼-inch-thick rounds
1 tablespoon plus 1½ teaspoons sea salt,
    divided
2 large russet potatoes, peeled
6 tablespoons extra-virgin olive oil, divided
1 medium yellow onion, chopped
1½ pounds lean ground beef
½ cup dry white wine
3 to 4 ripe medium tomatoes, chopped
1 tablespoon tomato paste diluted in
    ¼ cup water
2 tablespoons chopped fresh Italian
    flat-leaf parsley
¾ teaspoons freshly ground black pepper
1 recipe *Béchamel Sauce* (page 71)
¾ cup bread crumbs
½ cup grated kefalotiri *or* Parmesan cheese
½ cup brine-packed Greek feta, crumbled

Preheat oven to 400 degrees. Line 2 large baking sheets with foil or unbleached parchment paper. Lightly oil a 9 × 13-inch baking dish.

In a large mixing bowl, toss the eggplant with 1 tablespoon of the salt. Transfer to a large colander and sprinkle any salt left in the bowl over the top of the eggplant. Set a small plate on top of the eggplant and put a weight (such as a large can of tomatoes) on top of the plate to help squeeze out more water. Set the colander in the sink to drain for 30 minutes.

Meanwhile, boil the potatoes in a large pot of liberally salted water for 13 to 15 minutes. Make sure they are still firm enough to slice without crumbling to pieces. Lift the potatoes out with a slotted spoon and run under a gentle stream of cold water until cool enough to handle. Slice into ¼- to ½-inch rounds and set aside.

Rinse the eggplant well and pat dry with paper towels. Arrange the eggplant slices evenly in 1 layer on the prepared baking sheets. With a large pastry brush, very lightly brush the eggplant with 4 tablespoons of the olive oil. You may not need all of the oil. Bake for 15 to 20 minutes or until lightly browned, flipping the eggplant halfway through baking. Monitor closely so the eggplant does not burn. Remove from oven, and set aside. Reduce oven temperature to 350 degrees.

To make the meat sauce, heat the remaining 2 tablespoons of olive oil in a large stockpot or Dutch oven set over medium-high heat. Add the onion and cook until it is translucent, about 4 to 5 minutes. Add the ground beef, breaking up any large pieces with a spatula or wooden spoon, and cook until the meat is browned, 6 to 7 minutes. Add the white wine, chopped tomatoes, diluted tomato paste, parsley, remaining 1½ teaspoons of salt, and pepper. Stir to combine well, bring to a boil, reduce heat, and simmer until all the liquid has evaporated, about 10 minutes. Set aside.

To assemble the *moussaka*: Prepare the *Béchamel Sauce* according to the directions on page 71. Arrange all the sliced potatoes in an even layer at the bottom of the prepared baking dish. Cover the potatoes with half of the eggplant slices, arranged in even rows. Gently spread all of the meat sauce over the top of the eggplant. Top the meat sauce with half of the bread crumbs and half of the cheeses. Cover the bread crumb–cheese layer with the remaining eggplant slices, again arranged in even rows. Top the eggplant with the remaining bread crumbs and cheeses. Pour the *Béchamel Sauce* evenly over the top of the entire dish.

Bake for 55 to 60 minutes until heated through and the top begins to brown in spots, monitoring closely to ensure the top does not burn. Remove from oven, let cool for 10 minutes, slice, and serve.

Pastichio *(pah-STEE-chee-oh)*

This homey, decadent lasagna-style dish is the ultimate Greek comfort food, and it is definitely something I enjoy only once in a while! Depending on the region of Greece where you find yourself, some cooks may add cinnamon to *pastichio* and to many other dishes. I fall into the no-cinnamon camp, but if you love cinnamon, give it a shot.

SERVES 8

4 tablespoons extra-virgin olive oil, divided

1 medium yellow onion, finely chopped

1½ pounds lean ground lamb (or ground beef)

½ cup white wine

3 to 4 medium tomatoes, peeled and diced

1 tablespoon tomato paste diluted in 1 tablespoon warm water

1 tablespoon finely chopped fresh Italian flat-leaf parsley

2 teaspoons sea salt

1½ teaspoons freshly ground pepper

¼ teaspoon ground cinnamon (optional)

1½ cups hard barrel feta, coarsely grated (or brine-packed Greek feta, crumbled small), divided

1½ cups grated kefalotiri *or* Parmesan cheese, divided

1 pound pastichio pasta, penne, *or* ziti

1 recipe *Béchamel Sauce* (page 71)

4 large eggs, separated, 2 yolks reserved for *Béchamel Sauce*

To make the meat sauce: Heat 3 tablespoons of the olive oil in a large pot over medium heat. Add the onion and cook until lightly browned, 8 to 10 minutes, stirring occasionally. Add the lamb or beef and cook until no longer pink and lightly browned, about 10 minutes more, breaking up any large chunks with a spoon. Stir in the white wine, tomatoes, diluted tomato paste, parsley, salt, pepper, and cinnamon (if using). Increase heat to medium-high, bring to a boil, reduce heat to low, and simmer, uncovered, for 15 to 20 minutes or until the liquid has reduced to a thick sauce. Remove from heat, add ⅓ of the feta cheese and ⅓ of the kefalotiri or Parmesan cheese, and stir to combine. Set aside.

Boil the pasta in a large pot of salted water until it is slightly undercooked. The pasta will continue to cook in the oven, so take care not to overcook. Drain well in a colander, and toss with the remaining 1 tablespoon of olive oil.

Preheat oven to 350 degrees. Lightly oil a 9 × 13-inch baking dish. While the pasta is cooking, make the *Béchamel Sauce*, using 2 of the reserved egg yolks.

Layer half of the pasta into the prepared baking dish. Beat the 4 egg whites until slightly fluffy. Pour the beaten egg whites over the pasta. Evenly sprinkle half the remaining cheeses over the pasta. Evenly spread all of the meat sauce over the first layer of pasta. Top with the remaining pasta and pour the *Béchamel Sauce* evenly over the top layer. Top with the remaining cheeses. Bake for 50 to 60 minutes, until browned in spots, monitoring closely to ensure the top does not burn. Cool for 15 to 20 minutes before serving.

YIAYIA'S TIP: Don't waste those extra egg yolks! They'll keep in the refrigerator for up to 4 days.

Olokliri Kota sti Skara *(oh-LOH-klee-ree KOH-tah stee SKAH-rah)*

PERFECT HERB-ROASTED CHICKEN AND VEGETABLES

A good recipe for roasted chicken is a great addition to anyone's repertoire. This recipe can be doubled easily and yields an amazingly moist and flavorful chicken along with vegetables for a complete dinner.

SERVES 4 TO 6

1 roasting chicken, 4½ to 6 pounds

2½ teaspoons sea salt, divided

1 teaspoon freshly ground black pepper, divided

1 tablespoon lemon zest (1 lemon)

4 large lemons (1 of them zested)

10 sprigs fresh Italian flat-leaf parsley

10 sprigs fresh thyme

6 cloves garlic, smashed and peeled, divided

¾ cup roughly chopped fresh Italian
   flat-leaf parsley

¼ cup fresh thyme leaves

1 tablespoon dried oregano

⅓ cup extra-virgin olive oil

2 medium yellow onions, cut into thick slices

3 carrots, scrubbed clean, cut into
   1½-inch chunks

1 large fennel bulb (or 2 small), tops removed
   and sliced into wedges

Preheat oven to 425 degrees.

Thoroughly rinse the chicken under cold water, inside and out, removing any stray feathers and giblets. Pat the chicken very dry inside and out with paper towels. Tuck the wing tips under the body. Season the cavity with ½ teaspoon of the salt and ¼ teaspoon of the pepper. Slice the zested lemon in half, and place in the cavity along with the parsley and thyme sprigs and 3 cloves of the garlic. Tie the legs together with kitchen twine. Set chicken aside at room temperature.

Add the remaining 3 cloves of garlic, chopped parsley, thyme leaves, dried oregano, 1 teaspoon of the salt, and ½ teaspoon of the pepper to the bowl of a food processor. With the motor running, slowly pour in the olive oil until the mixture just comes together. Stir in the lemon zest. Alternatively, you can mash the garlic, seasonings, and oil together with a mortar and pestle. Set the herb mixture aside.

Distribute the onions, carrots, and fennel evenly onto the bottom of a large roasting pan, and season them with ½ teaspoon of the salt and ¼ teaspoon of the pepper. Slice 2 of the remaining lemons into large wedges and distribute them among the vegetables. Rub the chicken (top, bottom, sides) evenly with the herb mixture, making sure not to miss any nooks or crannies. For added measure, if desired, very carefully loosen the skin over the breast, and rub some of the herb mixture between the skin and the breast meat. Set the chicken on top of the vegetables in the pan and roast for 1½ hours or until the juices run clear when you make a small slice between a thigh and a leg.

Transfer the chicken and vegetables to a large serving dish, and cover with foil to rest for

20 minutes so that the juices can settle. After 20 minutes, remove the foil, cut the twine around the legs, and discard the contents of the cavity.

Carve the chicken and serve it with the vegetables and the remaining lemon cut into wedges for garnish.

Arni kai Patates (ahr-NEE keh pah-tah-TES)

CLASSIC ROASTED LEG OF LAMB WITH POTATOES

Although I was a vegetarian for twelve years, I still craved lamb. I have such fond memories of my father roasting a whole lamb on a spit in our backyard, which is very traditional for Greek Easter. Chances are you don't have enough space or time to roast an *entire* lamb, so try this recipe for roasted *leg* of lamb, which is just as juicy and delectable.

SERVES 6 TO 8

½ cup freshly squeezed lemon juice (3 to
   4 lemons)
¼ cup plus 2 tablespoons extra-virgin olive oil
1 tablespoon finely chopped fresh rosemary, plus
   16 individual leaves, divided
1 tablespoon dried oregano
1 tablespoon plus ½ teaspoon sea salt, divided
1¼ teaspoons freshly ground black pepper,
   divided
4 to 5 pounds small new potatoes (about 15 to
   20 potatoes), scrubbed clean and dried
1 bone-in leg of lamb, 7 to 8 pounds, aitchbone
   removed by butcher, rinsed, patted dry, fat
   trimmed to ¼-inch thick
4 cloves garlic, peeled and sliced into quarters

Whisk together the lemon juice, ¼ cup of the olive oil, the chopped rosemary, oregano, 1 tablespoon of the salt, and 1 teaspoon of the pepper. Set aside.

Lightly oil a large roasting pan. Add the potatoes to the pan and toss them with 2 tablespoons of the olive oil and the remaining ½ teaspoon of salt and ¼ teaspoon of pepper.

Make 16 evenly distributed ¾-inch-deep slits in the lamb (covering both sides) with a sharp paring knife. Insert a slice of garlic and 1 leaf of the rosemary into each slit. Place the leg of lamb, fat side up, on top of the potatoes. Spread the herb mixture all over the lamb, allowing any excess to drip down and coat the potatoes. Set aside to rest at room temperature for 30 minutes.

Preheat oven to 425 degrees.

Roast lamb and potatoes for 20 minutes at 425 degrees, then reduce oven temperature to 350 degrees. Continue to cook until a meat thermometer inserted 2 inches into the thickest part of the roast (do not touch the bone) reads between 135 and 140 degrees (medium rare), about 1½ to 2 hours. Baste every 20 minutes with the pan juices.

When the lamb is done, remove the pan from oven, and transfer the meat to a large cutting

(recipe continues)

board or platter. Cover with aluminum foil and set aside to rest for 20 minutes before carving. Meanwhile, transfer the potatoes to a serving bowl and cover them with foil. Pour the pan juices into a glass measuring cup. Skim and discard any fat that floats to the surface. Keep the juices warm while the lamb rests, adding any juices that drip from the resting meat to the measuring cup.

Carve the lamb, slicing against the grain. Serve with the potatoes, drizzled with the reserved pan juices (reheated if necessary).

Hirino Krassato *(hee-ree-NOH krah-SAH-toh)*

PORK IN WHITE WINE SAUCE

During the fall and winter seasons, Greeks love to enjoy comfort foods that warm them from the inside out. This typical country village dish is no exception.

SERVES 4

1½ pounds lean pork loin, cut into 4 (2-inch-thick) pieces

1½ teaspoons sea salt

1 teaspoon freshly ground black pepper

⅓ cup extra-virgin olive oil

½ cup white wine

1 cup warm water

1 recipe *Pilafi* (page 230) *or Kritharaki me Domata kai Feta* (page 180, omit feta) (optional)

Rinse the pork and pat dry with paper towels. Season with the salt and pepper.

Heat the olive oil in a large sauté pan over medium heat. Add the pork and sear, turning to brown on all sides, about 6 to 7 minutes total. When the meat is browned all over, add the wine and water, scraping up any brown bits stuck to the bottom of the pan.

Turn the heat up to medium-high and bring to a boil. Reduce heat to low, cover, and simmer for 20 minutes or until the meat is cooked through and beginning to fall apart. Serve over *Pilafi* or *Kritharaki me Domata kai Feta* (omit feta) if desired.

Soutzoukakia *(soo-zoo-KAH-kee-ah)*

GREEK MEATBALLS IN TOMATO SAUCE

These little delights remind me of my grand-mother, Thespena, for whom I am named. Her *soutzoukakia* were magical, and even though my mom and my aunts use the exact same ingredients, they have yet to replicate the flavor and texture of Yiayia's. I still wonder if she had a secret ingredient she never divulged. Still, this is her recipe, and it will yield a fantastic result—secret ingredient or not!

SERVES 4 TO 6

FOR THE TOMATO SAUCE

2 tablespoons extra-virgin olive oil
5 ripe medium tomatoes, seeded and diced
¼ teaspoons ground cumin
½ teaspoon sea salt
¼ teaspoon freshly ground black pepper

FOR THE MEATBALLS

1 to 1½ cups day-old bread, crusts removed, cubed
1½ pounds lean ground beef, extra ground
3 cloves garlic, finely chopped
¼ teaspoon ground cumin
¾ teaspoon sea salt
½ teaspoon freshly ground black pepper
1 recipe *Pilafi* (page 230) (optional)

To make the tomato sauce: Heat the olive oil over medium heat in a large pot or Dutch oven. Add the tomatoes, cumin, salt, and pepper. Cook over medium heat, stirring every so often, until the tomatoes break down, about 5 to 7 minutes. Reduce heat to low and simmer for 15 to 20 minutes, until the sauce has thickened slightly.

Preheat oven to 350 degrees. Lightly oil a large baking dish.

To make the meatballs: Soak the bread briefly in a bowl of water, just to wet it all the way through. Squeeze the water from the bread, and transfer to a large mixing bowl. Use impeccably clean hands to gently mix the remaining meatball ingredients together until thoroughly combined.

Roll the meat mixture into little sausage shapes, about 2 inches long. Carefully arrange the meatballs in the prepared baking dish in an even layer. Bake for 35 minutes.

Remove the meatballs from the oven and immediately add them to the tomato sauce, taking care not to break them. Gently stir to coat the meatballs in the sauce and cook for 5 minutes more over low heat. Serve over *Pilafi,* if desired.

Lemonati kai Reganati Kota

(leh-moh-NAH-tee keh ree-ghah-NAH-tee KOH-tah)

LEMON AND OREGANO CHICKEN BREASTS

This Greek twist on a basic baked chicken breast is one of my favorite fast and simple, go-to weeknight meals. These chicken breasts are also delicious served cold the next day over a green salad. Serve them hot with *Lemonates Patates* (page 240) for a totally satisfying and delicious Greek take on the classic chicken and potatoes dinner.

SERVES 4

2 to 3 tablespoons freshly squeezed lemon juice
    (1 lemon)
¼ cup extra-virgin olive oil
1 teaspoon sea salt
½ teaspoon freshly ground black pepper
1 teaspoon dried oregano
4 skinless, boneless chicken breasts, washed well
    and patted dry

In a medium mixing bowl, whisk together the lemon juice, olive oil, salt, pepper, and oregano. Transfer the mixture to a large Ziploc bag and add the chicken. Squeeze out as much air as possible, seal the bag, and shake to coat the chicken in the marinade. Place in the refrigerator for 1 hour, turning once after 30 minutes.

Preheat oven to 350 degrees. Lightly oil a 9 × 13-inch baking dish.

Transfer the chicken to the prepared baking dish and pour the marinade over the top. Cover tightly with aluminum foil and bake in preheated oven for 20 to 25 minutes or until the juices run clear. Uncover and bake for 5 more minutes. Remove from oven and allow the chicken to cool and rest for 5 to 10 minutes. Serve warm.

Kritharaki me Kreas *(kree-thah-RAH-kee meh KREH-ahs)*

ORZO AND BEEF CASSEROLE

During the cold winter months, this casserole was a Sunday institution in our house. It reminds me of football season because the whole family would gather in the kitchen cooking and watching Sunday football.

SERVES 4 TO 6

2½ pounds boneless beef chuck, cut into 4 to 6 large pieces

½ cup plus 2 tablespoons extra-virgin olive oil, divided

2 teaspoons sea salt

1½ teaspoons freshly ground black pepper

½ teaspoon garlic powder

1 teaspoon dried oregano

4 cups water, divided

4 to 5 very ripe medium tomatoes, chopped

¼ cup finely chopped yellow onion

2 cloves garlic, finely minced

1 tablespoon tomato paste

1½ cups orzo

Rinse the beef, and pat dry with a paper towel.

Heat 2 tablespoons of the olive oil over medium heat in a large oven-safe stockpot or Dutch oven. Add the beef and sprinkle the salt, pepper, garlic powder, and oregano over it. Slowly sear the beef, turning it every 2 to 4 minutes to brown on all sides, about 10 to 14 minutes total. Add 1 cup of the water and bring to a simmer. Reduce heat to low, cover, and cook for 20 minutes.

Preheat oven to 350 degrees.

Add the tomatoes, onion, and garlic to the beef. Stir to combine, cover, and cook for 10 minutes more. Mix the tomato paste into the remaining 3 cups of water. Add the tomato paste–water mixture, orzo, and remaining ½ cup olive oil to the pot, and stir to combine. Cover, transfer to the oven, and bake for 30 minutes. Serve immediately.

Lahano me Kreas *(LAH-hah-noh meh KREH-ahs)*

SPICY CABBAGE AND PORK STEW

This traditional stew was my one of my dad's favorite dinnertime meals. He loved the spiciness of the chili pepper. Not for the faint of heart, this dish has a real kick, especially if you happen to swallow a larger piece of chili. Years ago at a family dinner, I actually thought I had burned my esophagus. By the way, should that happen to you, the simplest cure is cold Greek yogurt, which cools the burning sensation almost immediately. If you are not a fan of the heat, you can omit the chili pepper.

SERVES 6

2½ pounds boneless lean pork shoulder, cut into
    1-inch cubes
1½ teaspoons sea salt
½ teaspoon freshly ground black pepper
3 tablespoons extra-virgin olive oil
½ cup white wine
1 medium onion, chopped
1½ cups *Mama's Domata Saltsa* (page 74) *or*
    1 14.5-ounce can stewed tomatoes
2 tablespoons tomato paste
2 carrots, chopped (optional)
1 clove garlic, finely chopped
1 teaspoon finely chopped fresh oregano
1 cup water
1 whole head cabbage, cored and cut into strips
1 small fresh chili pepper, diced (optional)

Rinse the pork, and pat dry with paper towels. Season the pork all over with the salt and pepper. Heat the olive oil in a large stockpot or Dutch oven set over medium heat. Add the pork cubes and brown them on all sides, turning them every minute or two for about 6 to 7 minutes total.

Add the white wine and scrape up any brown bits. Add the onion and cook until it starts to caramelize, about 6 to 8 minutes, stirring occasionally. Add the stewed tomatoes (with their liquid if using canned), tomato paste, carrots (if using), garlic, oregano, and water. Bring to a boil, then reduce heat to simmer. Add the cabbage and chili pepper (if using). Cover and simmer over low heat until the cabbage and meat are extremely tender, about 45 minutes.

Taste and adjust seasonings, if necessary. Serve immediately.

Lahanika kai Rizi
VEGETABLES AND RICE

At the Greek table, vegetables usually play the lead role. Greek cooks have mastered the art of taking a few simple ingredients from the earth and turning them into a symphony of tastes and textures. The rich soil of Greece lends itself to growing an incredible variety of glorious vegetables. In addition, restaurant chefs and home cooks alike choose vegetables that are grown locally and picked at the peak of ripeness. It is almost impossible to find a vegetable in a Greek market that is not sourced locally and picked at the peak of its season. Vegetables are nutrient dense, and many of their healing powers have yet to be fully understood. Still, when you look at the exemplary health and longevity of most of the Greek population, it is undeniable that they are doing something right. I spent many of my formative years in Greece, and I know firsthand the wealth of vegetables served at every meal. In fact, as I've mentioned before, farm-fresh vegetables cover the lion's share of a typical Greek plate. These vegetable recipes are some of my absolute favorites, and I encourage you to try them, even if you think you don't like a certain vegetable. You may just be surprised!

Bamies Lathera *(BAH-mee-ehs lah-theh-RAH)*

OKRA IN TOMATO SAUCE WITH ONION

Okra has a bad reputation for being a slimy character. But the truth of the matter is that it's slimy only when it's prepared incorrectly. After eating okra made this way, your opinion will change. Go ahead and give this often-maligned but truly delicious vegetable a second chance!

SERVES 4 TO 6

2 pounds fresh okra

½ cup red or white wine vinegar

2 teaspoons sea salt, divided, plus more to taste

1 cup extra-virgin olive oil

1 medium yellow onion, chopped

3 cloves garlic, finely chopped

3 or 4 very ripe medium tomatoes, peeled and chopped

1 tablespoon tomato paste diluted in 1 cup water

1 teaspoon honey

½ teaspoon freshly ground black pepper

Rinse the okra. As shown on the opposite page, carefully cut off the very tip of the stem with a paring knife, rounding the stem slightly as you cut. Take care not to remove the entire stem or the okra will become slimy. Transfer to a large mixing bowl.

Add enough water to the okra just to cover, along with the vinegar and 1 teaspoon of the salt. Stir very gently to combine. Put the bowl in a sunny place in the kitchen for 2 to 3 hours. After at least 2 hours, lift the okra out of the vinegar solution a few at a time and squeeze over the sink, pressing firmly enough that the gelatinous matter drains out but gently enough not to break or crush the okra pod. Transfer the okra to a large colander and rinse under cold water. Set aside.

Heat the olive oil over medium heat in a large sauté pan. Add the onion and sauté until translucent, 4 to 5 minutes, stirring frequently. Add the garlic and cook for 1 minute more. Add the tomatoes, tomato paste–water mixture, and honey, and stir to combine. Increase heat to medium-high, bring to a boil, and reduce heat to low. Simmer, stirring occasionally, for 5 minutes.

Add 1 cup of water, the remaining 1 teaspoon of salt, and the pepper to the sauté pan. Stir again to combine. Add the okra and stir once, very gently. Do not stir again. Cover and cook over low heat for 40 minutes, or until most of the liquid has evaporated.

Remove from heat, uncover, and let cool for a few minutes. Taste and adjust seasonings, if necessary. Transfer to a serving dish and serve immediately.

— ⚑ —

DEBBIE'S TIP: Raw okra can cause a mild allergic reaction in sensitive people. You may want to wear rubber gloves while cleaning raw okra, especially if your hands start to itch.

Oven-Baked Okra

This oven-baked variation of *Bamies Lathera* (page 224) is just as delicious as the original. Baking the okra in the oven requires almost no effort and yields a more attractive finished dish.

SERVES 4 TO 6

2 to 3 tablespoons extra-virgin olive oil, plus more for baking dish

2 pounds fresh okra

½ cup red or white wine vinegar

2 teaspoons sea salt, divided, plus more to taste

1 medium yellow onion, chopped

3 cloves garlic, finely chopped

3 or 4 very ripe medium tomatoes, peeled and chopped

¼ cup chopped fresh Italian flat-leaf parsley

½ teaspoon freshly ground black pepper (optional)

Preheat oven to 350 degrees. Oil a 9 × 13-inch baking dish.

Trim, soak, squeeze, drain, and rinse the okra as directed on page 224.

Place half the prepared okra in the bottom of the baking dish in an even layer. Evenly distribute half of the onion, garlic, tomatoes, parsley, remaining salt, and pepper (if using). Follow with the remaining okra and then with the remaining vegetables and spices (if using). Slowly drizzle the olive oil over the top.

Bake, covered, for 30 minutes. Uncover and bake for 1 hour more. Serve immediately.

Araka Lathera (ah-rah-KAH lah-theh-RAH)

PEAS WITH TOMATOES IN OLIVE OIL

So many dishes in Greece are prepared *lathera* style, which simply means cooked with tomatoes and olive oil. And truthfully, what could be more delicious? I cannot think of a better way to get kids to eat their peas! Try this method with your favorite fresh, seasonal vegetables.

SERVES 4 TO 6

2 pounds fresh or frozen English peas, shelled
    if necessary
¾ cup extra-virgin olive oil
6 to 7 scallions, white parts thinly sliced, green
    parts cut into ⅛-inch slices
¾ pound very ripe tomatoes, peeled and sliced
    into wedges
3 tablespoons finely chopped fresh dill
1½ teaspoons sea salt
½ teaspoon freshly ground pepper
3 to 4 cups water

Rinse the peas in a colander and set aside.

Heat the olive oil in a large saucepan set over medium heat. Add the sliced scallions and sauté until they start to brown, 5 to 6 minutes, stirring frequently. Add the peas and stir to combine. Keep a close eye on the peas and continue to stir them gently until they begin to brown slightly, 5 to 6 minutes more. Stir in the tomatoes, dill, salt, and pepper. Pour in 3 cups of the water, until peas are halfway submerged, adding more water if necessary. Increase heat to medium-high, bring to a boil, and reduce heat to simmer. Cook, covered, for 35 minutes or until nearly all liquid has evaporated, checking occasionally to ensure the peas do not burn. Serve immediately.

Fassolakia Yiahni *(fah-soh-LAH-kee-ah yahck-NEE)*

GREEN BEANS BRAISED WITH TOMATOES AND ONIONS

If you've been perusing this book, you have probably noticed that Greeks use a lot of tomatoes and olive oil in their cooking. *Lathera* style means that a dish is cooked with tomatoes and olive oil; *yiahni* style adds onions to the mix. These green beans, cooked *yiahni* style with tomatoes and onions, are especially scrumptious.

SERVES 4 TO 6

1 cup extra-virgin olive oil, divided

1 large yellow onion, chopped

1 clove garlic, minced

1½ pounds fresh green beans, washed and trimmed

3 ripe medium tomatoes, peeled and chopped

1 tablespoon tomato paste diluted in 2 cups water

½ cup finely chopped fresh Italian flat-leaf parsley

1 teaspoon sea salt, plus more to taste

½ teaspoon freshly ground black pepper, plus more to taste

Heat ½ cup of the olive oil in a large pot over medium heat. Add the onion and sauté until it just begins to brown, about 7 to 8 minutes, stirring frequently. Add the garlic and cook 1 minute more. Reduce heat to low and add the green beans. Cover and cook for 10 minutes.

Stir in the tomatoes and the diluted tomato paste. If the mixture seems dry, add a bit more water, to cover the beans halfway. Stir in the remaining ½ cup of the olive oil and the parsley. Increase heat to medium-high, bring to a boil, and reduce heat to a simmer. Cook, covered, for 40 minutes, until most of the water has evaporated and the sauce has thickened.

Add the salt and pepper, remove from heat, and let cool for a few minutes while the flavors meld.

Taste and adjust seasonings, if necessary, before serving.

Pilafi *(pee-LAH-fee)*

RICE PILAF WITH CARROTS AND PARSLEY

I have yet to meet anyone who does not love a good rice pilaf! It pairs well with almost anything and is so easy to make. This version is a go-to favorite when I am entertaining because all you have to do is throw it in the oven and set the timer while you work on other things. Thirty minutes later, you've got a great side dish, and you didn't have to babysit it on the stove. I love simplifying life!

SERVES 4 TO 6

1½ cups long-grain white rice
2 tablespoons extra-virgin olive oil
1 medium yellow onion, finely chopped
2 carrots, diced
1 bay leaf
2¾ cups low-sodium vegetable or chicken broth
½ teaspoon sea salt, plus more to taste
½ cup finely chopped fresh Italian flat-leaf parsley

Preheat oven to 375 degrees. Rinse the rice very well in a fine-mesh sieve.

Heat the olive oil over medium heat in a large oven-safe stockpot or Dutch oven. Add the onion, carrots, and bay leaf. Sauté until the onion is translucent and the carrots begin to soften, about 4 to 5 minutes, stirring constantly. Add the rice, stirring to coat it in the oil, and cook until the rice turns an opaque white, about 2 minutes.

Pour in the broth and add the salt. Increase heat to medium-high and bring to a boil. Stir once, cover the pot, and transfer it to the oven.

Bake for 30 minutes or until the rice is tender and all the liquid has been absorbed. If making ahead, the pilaf will hold in the turned-off oven for 30 minutes. When ready to serve, remove from the oven, add the parsley, and gently fluff the rice with a fork.

Taste and adjust seasonings, if necessary. Transfer the pilaf to a large serving dish or wide bowl, and serve.

———————— 🇬🇷 ————————

YIAYIA'S TIP: If you don't have a pot that goes from stovetop to oven, prepare the recipe in a large saucepan and transfer it to a lightly oiled baking dish after you stir in the broth and salt. Cover with aluminum foil, and bake as directed.

Kolokithia Lathera *(koh-loh-KEE-thee-ah lah-theh-RAH)*

STEWED ZUCCHINI WITH TOMATOES AND OLIVE OIL

Zucchini is one of the most popular vegetables in all of Greece. Whether it is zucchini fritters, stuffed zucchini, fried zucchini, *kolokithopita,* or simply stewed, Greeks eat zucchini in some form several times per week. This zucchini dish, cooked *lathera* style, is both simple and scrumptious.

SERVES 4 TO 6

1½ pounds fresh zucchini

1 cup extra-virgin olive oil

2 yellow onions, finely chopped

4 ripe medium tomatoes, peeled and sliced into large wedges

1 tablespoon tomato paste diluted in 1 cup water

3 cloves garlic, finely chopped

2 tablespoons finely chopped fresh Italian flat-leaf parsley

2 teaspoons sea salt, plus more to taste

½ teaspoon freshly ground black pepper

1 cup water

With a large kitchen knife, slice each zucchini in half lengthwise, and then cut each half into 2-inch chunks. Set aside.

Heat the olive oil in a large pot set over medium heat. Sauté the onion until lightly browned, about 8 to 10 minutes, stirring frequently. Add the tomatoes, tomato paste–water mixture, and garlic. Increase heat to medium-high, bring to a boil, and reduce heat to a simmer. Add the zucchini, parsley, salt, pepper, and water. Cover and cook over medium-low heat for 20 to 25 minutes, or until nearly all the liquid has evaporated.

Taste and adjust seasonings, if necessary, before serving.

Kounoupithi Vrasto *(koo-noo-PEE-thee vrah-STOH)*

CAULIFLOWER IN THE CLASSIC GREEK STYLE

It's hard to believe something so simple can be so flavorful. With four main ingredients—cauliflower, olive oil, lemon juice, and salt—you have a vegetable dish fit for a Greek god or goddess!

SERVES 4 TO 6

3 tablespoons plus ½ teaspoon sea salt, plus more to taste

1 large head cauliflower, washed, stemmed, green leaves removed, and cut into florets

2 to 3 tablespoons freshly squeezed lemon juice (about 1 lemon)

2 to 3 tablespoons extra-virgin olive oil

1 lemon, sliced into large wedges, for garnish (optional)

Bring water to a boil in a large pot set over medium-high heat. Stir in 3 tablespoons of the salt and gently lower the cauliflower into the water, cover, and cook for 3 to 4 minutes or until it is crisp tender, being careful not to overcook. The water may not return a full boil before the cauliflower is done.

When the cauliflower is crisp tender, carefully lift it out of the water using a large slotted spoon or a fine-mesh strainer, and transfer it to a large mixing bowl. In a small bowl, quickly whisk together the lemon juice, olive oil, and remaining ½ teaspoon of salt. While the cauliflower is piping hot, toss gently with the dressing.

Serve immediately with the lemon wedges, if desired.

Oven-Roasted Broccoli with Lemon

Although broccoli is seldom served in Greece, you can still find it, most often the purple variety. Still, my family ate a lot of broccoli when I was growing up in Virginia. This is my mom's roasted broccoli with Greek flavors. It's amazing what a little lemon and garlic can do for a vegetable.

SERVES 2 TO 4

12 to 14 ounces broccoli florets, washed and
  dried well
2 tablespoons extra-virgin olive oil
¼ teaspoon sea salt
¼ teaspoon freshly ground black pepper
⅛ teaspoon garlic powder (optional)
2 tablespoons freshly squeezed lemon juice
  (1 lemon)

Preheat oven to 400 degrees. Line a large baking sheet with unbleached parchment paper.

Place the broccoli on the prepared baking sheet, drizzle with the olive oil, and season with the salt, pepper, and garlic powder (if using). Give the broccoli a quick toss with impeccably clean hands, then spread it in an even layer. Bake until the broccoli is bright green and the tips are slightly charred, about 10 minutes. Remove from oven and dress with the lemon juice.

Serve immediately.

Roasted Red Bliss Potatoes with Garlic, Oregano, and Lemon

These potatoes are amazing! I serve them with soup, fish, or chicken and sometimes along with broccoli for an easy and quick veggie dinner. Garlic powder is a great trick here because you don't have to chop it, and it doesn't burn at high heat, which makes these potatoes very low maintenance. When I am having guests over, I love quick-to-prepare side dishes that just go in the oven and come out perfect. These are great hot out of the oven or served cold the next day.

SERVES 4 TO 6

3 pounds skin-on red bliss potatoes, scrubbed, dried, and cut into 1½-inch chunks
3 tablespoons extra-virgin olive oil
1½ teaspoons garlic powder
1½ teaspoons dried oregano
1½ teaspoons sea salt
¾ teaspoon freshly ground black pepper
2 teaspoons lemon zest
¼ cup freshly squeezed lemon juice (2 lemons)

Preheat oven to 400 degrees. Line 2 large baking sheets with unbleached parchment paper.

Divide the potatoes equally between the prepared baking sheets. Drizzle them with the olive oil and sprinkle them with the garlic powder, oregano, salt, and pepper. Give the potatoes a quick toss with impeccably clean hands to distribute the seasonings and coat with the oil, and spread them evenly into a single layer on each baking sheet. Be sure not to position them too close to one another, or they will steam rather than roast.

Bake for 45 to 50 minutes, stirring gently after 20 minutes, until the potatoes are golden brown and crispy on the outside and soft on the inside.

Sprinkle the lemon zest and lemon juice over the hot potatoes, mix gently, and serve.

YIAYIA'S TIP: Don't overdo it with the oil or your potatoes will be greasy instead of crispy!

Simply Minted Peas

Mint and peas are a totally amazing combination. Something about the combination works perfectly. Serve these peas with whatever you like—they go with almost anything!

SERVES 4

1 tablespoon butter or extra-virgin olive oil, plus more as needed

2 cups fresh English peas, shelled and blanched (see tip), or 2 cups frozen

1½ teaspoons finely chopped fresh mint

¼ teaspoon sea salt

¼ teaspoon freshly ground black pepper

Melt the butter or heat the olive oil in a small saucepan over medium-low heat. Add the peas and stir to heat through, adding a touch more butter or oil if the peas start sticking. When the peas are hot, add the mint, salt, and pepper.

Taste and adjust seasonings, if necessary. Serve immediately.

———————— 🇬🇷 ————————

DEBBIE'S TIP: I love to use frozen peas because they're convenient and always available, and you can use them straight from the freezer. However, when fresh peas are in season, you can't beat their sweet and delicate flavor. If you're using fresh peas, shell them, cook for 2 minutes in boiling, salted water, then cool quickly by transferring to a sieve and running under cold water.

Spanakorizo *(spah-nah-KOH-ree-zoh)*

SPINACH RICE

Every Greek mom has her own special twist on this traditional rice dish. Some add certain herbs and spices while others add entirely different seasonings. I have even seen this dish made with tomatoes. All are delicious, but as you might expect, I'm partial to my mom's.

SERVES 4 TO 6

½ cup extra-virgin olive oil

3 scallions, white and soft green parts
   thinly sliced

1 medium yellow onion, chopped

2 pounds fresh spinach, coarse stems removed,
   washed in several changes of cold water,
   drained, and chopped

2½ cups water, divided

1⅓ cups long-grain white rice

2 tablespoons finely chopped fresh dill

1 tablespoon finely chopped fresh parsley

1 teaspoon sea salt

¼ teaspoon freshly ground black pepper

3 tablespoons freshly squeezed lemon juice (about
   1 to 1½ lemons)

Heat the olive oil in a large stockpot or Dutch oven over medium heat and sauté the scallion and the onion until translucent but not browned, about 5 to 6 minutes, stirring frequently. Add the spinach and 1 cup of the water, and cook until the spinach wilts, about 5 minutes. If your pot is not large enough to accommodate all the uncooked spinach at once, add the spinach in stages, allowing it to wilt down slightly for a couple of minutes before adding more.

Add the rice, dill, parsley, salt, pepper, and remaining 1½ cups of water. Increase heat to medium-high, and bring to a boil. Reduce heat to a simmer, stir once, cover, and cook for exactly 20 minutes. Do not overcook and do not stir while the rice is simmering. After 20 minutes, remove from heat and let stand for 5 minutes, covered.

Uncover, fluff rice with a fork, and gently stir in the lemon juice. Cover again and cook over very low heat for another 5 minutes. Remove from heat and let stand, covered, for 15 to 20 more minutes so that all the flavors fully come together.

Serve immediately.

Lemonates Patates *(leh-moh-NAH-tehs pah-tah-TES)*

LEMON POTATOES

This is a very easy and tasty way to change up your family's typical potato recipe. These potatoes are so flavorful, you will not believe how quickly they come together. In my house, my mom would put a full baking dish into the oven, but it would come out half empty because my brother, sister, and I would sneak into the kitchen, open the oven, and filch a few slices at a time. My favorites are the ones that are extra browned and crunchy on top.

SERVES 6

½ cup extra-virgin olive oil, plus more for baking dish

1½ pounds Yukon Gold potatoes, peeled and cut into 4 to 6 wedges each

1 teaspoon sea salt

1 teaspoon yellow mustard (such as French's)

½ cup warm water

2 to 3 tablespoons freshly squeezed lemon juice (1 lemon)

½ teaspoon freshly ground black pepper (optional)

Preheat oven to 350 degrees. Lightly oil a 9 × 13-inch baking dish.

Place the potatoes in the baking dish, season with the salt, and toss to combine with impeccably clean hands.

In a small mixing bowl, whisk the mustard together with the warm water, lemon juice, and olive oil. Pour the mustard mixture evenly over the potatoes. Toss the potatoes again to make sure they are well coated. Spread them in an even layer, and season with the pepper (if using).

Cover with aluminum foil and bake for 40 minutes. Uncover and bake until golden, 15 to 20 minutes more.

Serve immediately.

READING DEBBIE'S COFFEE CUP

In the mountain city of Xanthi, where my family is from, lives a woman named Anastasia who specializes in reading the coffee grounds left at the bottom of a cup of traditional Greek coffee. She and I were introduced by a mutual friend, and I decided to let her have a crack at my cup. This ancient art of foretelling one's future is similar in principle to reading one's tea leaves. The idea is that when you drink from the coffee cup, your soul leaves a fingerprint of sorts on the cup, and the leftover coffee grinds identify the pattern of that fingerprint. Like so many traditions in Greece, the art of reading coffee

grinds is taught and passed down from generation to generation and historically, was practiced exclusively by women. Believe it or not, in the olden days, reading cups was considered so taboo that if a woman were discovered doing so, she could be barred from attending church services until she publicly repented. Today, the reading of coffee cups is still done only by women, and while frowned upon by the devoutly religious, it is more in good fun than anything else. Still, every time I have had my coffee cup read, the insights seemed to be eerily accurate. . . . But then again, the same goes for my monthly horoscope!

Glyka
SWEET PASTRIES, CAKES, AND COOKIES

The American concept of dessert is foreign to Greeks. A typical Greek meal ends with a large plate of seasonal fresh fruit, which is shared by the table. Watermelon, sliced peaches, figs, cherries, and grapes are all great examples of fruit that might be served to wrap up a Greek meal. However, Greeks do enjoy elaborate cakes, sweet pastries, and cookies when company visits or when out for a stroll in town with a friend. These sweets are almost always accompanied by a small cup of strong Greek coffee and a tall, cold glass of water. Most Greek cakes and pastries are soaked in a lovely sugar or honey-based syrup typically flavored with lemon and cinnamon, and many contain or are topped with chopped walnuts.

Zaharoplastia, which translates directly to "sugar sculptures," are what Greeks call the boutique pastry shops that even Willy Wonka would envy. The master pastry chef owner of the shop is called a *zaharoplastis*, or sugar sculptor. A *zaharoplastis* is a true artisan, whose technique and ability to sculpt pastries are honed over time and passed down from generation to generation. Every town, city, and village in Greece contains *zaharoplastia* that specialize in regional favorites. There are hundreds of varieties of these gorgeous Greek confections. Unfortunately, I could choose only a few of my family's prized recipes for this book. I hope you enjoy them as we do . . . in moderation!

Baklava (bah-klah-VAH)

Here is my family's secret recipe for the best *Baklava* ever. Rolling it this way, as opposed to baking it in a flat pan, ensures a light flakiness and just the right amount of the honey syrup running throughout. Around the holiday season, when I was growing up, my mom would make big batches of this so that my sister, my brother, and I could give platters of it to our teachers. Needless to say, every new school year, teachers were very excited to see one of the Matenopoulos kids on their class rosters!

YIELDS APPROXIMATELY 39 PIECES

FOR THE *BAKLAVA*

1¼ pounds walnuts (about 5 cups), finely chopped

2 tablespoons granulated sugar

2 teaspoons ground cinnamon

1 (1-pound) package phyllo dough sheets
    (13 × 18 inches), thawed (see tip, page 112)
    (18 sheets)

1 cup (2 sticks) unsalted butter, melted

FOR THE SYRUP

2 cups sugar

2 cups water

1 cup honey

1 (2-inch-wide) piece fresh lemon peel

2 tablespoons freshly squeezed lemon juice
    (1 lemon)

Preheat oven to 325 degrees.

In a medium mixing bowl, stir together the walnuts, sugar, and cinnamon, and set aside.

Working quickly, and keeping the unused phyllo sheets covered, lay out 1 sheet of phyllo on a clean flat surface. Lightly brush the phyllo sheet with the melted butter. Cover with a second phyllo sheet and butter. Sprinkle about ½ cup of the nut mixture over the top sheet. Repeat this process with 2 more sheets of phyllo and another ½ cup of the nut mixture, then again with last 2 phyllo sheets and a final ½ cup of the nut mixture. You will have used 6 sheets of phyllo and 1½ cups of the nut mixture (3 layers). Starting at the long end (the 18-inch side), gently roll the layered phyllo sheets up into a tight, fat roll. Brush the seam with butter to seal. Repeat the entire process twice more. One package will make 3 rolls.

Using a large, very sharp knife, cut the rolls into 1-inch pieces. Lay the pieces cut side down on 2 large ungreased rimmed baking sheets. Bake for 20 minutes, remove from oven, and, using a large spatula or tongs, quickly flip the *baklava* over. Return to the oven and bake for 20 minutes more or until cooked through, golden and flaky.

While the *baklava* is baking, make the syrup. Combine all of the syrup ingredients except the lemon juice in a medium, nonreactive saucepan. Set it over medium-high heat, bring to a boil, reduce heat, and simmer for 12 minutes, stirring occasionally. After 12 minutes, stir in the lemon juice, and cook for 3 more minutes. Remove from heat and carefully remove and discard the lemon peel. Let the syrup cool slightly.

Remove the *baklava* from the oven and slowly pour the warm syrup over pieces on the baking sheets. Let stand 1 hour to soak up the syrup.

Transfer to individual cupcake wrappers, if desired, and serve. The *baklava* will keep, covered loosely, at room temperature for up to 1 week.

DEBBIE'S TIP: To make a vegan *baklava,* substitute a vegan butter (like Earth Balance Vegan Buttery Sticks) for the dairy butter, use maple sugar or organic (vegan) sugar, and omit the honey, if desired.

Karithopita *(kah-ree-THOH-pee-tah)*

CLASSIC WALNUT CAKE

Karithopita is a classic cake soaked, like so many Greek desserts, in a lightly spiced sugar syrup. This moist and delectable cake is great to make on a Sunday afternoon, as it will keep, covered, at room temperature for four to five days. Many Greek households keep this cake on hand to serve in case unexpected company drops by for coffee, which is truly a part of the Greek culture. A small piece makes a great afternoon snack or light dessert.

YIELDS 24 PIECES

FOR THE CAKE

3 cups walnut halves

½ cup (1 stick) unsalted butter, at room
    temperature

1 cup granulated sugar

4 large eggs

1 teaspoon pure vanilla extract

2 teaspoons freshly squeezed lemon juice

2 cups all-purpose flour

1 teaspoon baking soda

1½ teaspoons baking powder

¼ teaspoon sea salt

1 tablespoon ground cinnamon

½ cup milk

FOR THE SYRUP

2 cups water

2 cups sugar

1 (1-inch wide) slice lemon peel, 2 inches long

1 cinnamon stick

Preheat oven to 350 degrees. Butter and flour a 9 × 13-inch baking dish.

Process the walnuts in a food processor or high-performance blender, pulsing until they are coarsely ground. They should retain a slight texture, not become a very fine meal. Set aside.

In the bowl of an electric mixer fitted with the paddle attachment, beat together the butter and sugar on medium-high speed until light and fluffy, about 3 minutes. Reduce the speed to low and add the eggs, 1 at a time, beating well after each addition. Add the vanilla and lemon juice, and mix until combined. Pause to scrape down the sides of the bowl a couple of times during mixing.

In a separate bowl, whisk together the flour, baking soda, baking powder, salt, and cinnamon. Stir in the walnuts, coating them well in the flour. With the mixer running on low, add the flour mixture in thirds, alternating with the milk (adding half at a time in 2 additions), and ending with the flour mixture. Scrape down the sides of the bowl a couple of times during mixing, mixing only until just combined. Take care not to over-mix.

Transfer the batter to the prepared baking dish, and smooth the top with an offset spatula. Bake until the cake is golden brown and a wooden skewer or cake tester inserted into the center comes out clean, about 25 to 30 minutes. Let cool for 20 minutes.

While the cake is cooling, combine all of the syrup ingredients in a medium, nonreactive saucepan. Bring to a boil over medium-high heat, reduce heat, and simmer for 15 minutes, stirring frequently, until the mixture resembles a light maple syrup. Cool for 5 minutes, then carefully remove and discard the lemon peel and cinnamon stick.

Pour the hot syrup over the cooled cake and let stand at room temperature for 1 hour so that cake can soak up the syrup.

Cut the cake into 24 pieces and serve.

Kataifi *(kah-tah-EE-fee)*

ROLLED WALNUT-FILLED GREEK PASTRY IN SYRUP

Kataifi, or *kadaife,* is a special kind of Greek pastry. Made from flour and water, it is processed in such a way that when it dries, it forms long thin strands that resemble angel hair pasta or shredded wheat. You can find it frozen in Greek specialty stores and some gourmet food stores.

YIELDS 24 PIECES

FOR THE SYRUP

2 cups granulated sugar

2 cups water

1 cup honey

1 2-inch piece fresh lemon peel

2 tablespoons freshly squeezed lemon juice
    (1 lemon)

FOR THE ROLLS

2¼ cups coarsely chopped walnuts

¼ cup granulated sugar

1 teaspoon ground cinnamon

¼ teaspoon ground cloves

1 egg, lightly beaten

1 pound *kataifi,* thawed overnight in the
    refrigerator if frozen

1½ cups (3 sticks) unsalted butter, melted

To make the syrup, combine all the syrup ingredients except the lemon juice in a medium, nonreactive saucepan, and bring to a boil over medium-high heat. Reduce heat to low and simmer for 12 minutes, stirring occasionally. Stir in the lemon juice and cook for 3 minutes, until the mixture has the consistency of light maple syrup. Remove from heat and carefully remove and discard the lemon peel. Set aside to let cool slightly.

In a large mixing bowl, combine the walnuts, sugar, cinnamon, ground cloves, and egg, and mix well to combine. Set aside.

Preheat oven to 350 degrees. Lightly butter a large rimmed baking sheet.

Carefully roll out the *kataifi* dough onto a cool surface. Loosen and separate the strands into 24 separate long strips, each one 3 inches wide by 10 to 12 inches long. Working 1 piece at a time, place 1 heaping tablespoon of the walnut filling across the width of the dough at one end of each strip of dough. Roll up into a tight small roll, tucking in any stray pieces of dough as you roll and taking care not to break the dough. Transfer the roll to the prepared baking sheet, seam side down. Leave about a finger space between each roll so that they crisp in the oven. Continue until you have used up all the dough.

You should have 24 pieces. Spoon 1 tablespoon of the melted butter over each piece. Place in the preheated oven, and bake until golden, about 30 minutes. As soon as you remove the hot rolls from the oven, evenly pour all the cooled syrup over them. Cover loosely with aluminum foil, and cool for about 1 hour. If you prefer a softer texture, cover the rolls with plastic wrap, which will keep the pastry very moist. *Kataifi* will keep in an airtight container at room temperature for up to 4 days.

YIAYIA'S TIP: Like phyllo dough, *kataifi* dough dries out very quickly. Make sure all your ingredients are ready to go before you roll it out, and keep the unused portion covered with wax paper or plastic wrap, with a damp kitchen towel on top.

DEBBIE'S TIP: To make vegan *kataifi*, substitute a vegan butter (like Earth Balance Vegan Buttery Sticks) for the butter, use maple sugar or organic, vegan sugar, and omit the egg and honey, if desired.

Kourambiethes *(koo-rah-BEE-YEH-thehs)*

GREEK WEDDING COOKIES

Kourambiethes are served year-round at many holidays and special occasions in Greece. They are easy to prepare, buttery, and coated in powdered sugar, which gives them a lovely festive appearance. Their white color indicates wishes for continued happiness and good fortune. These cookies may take a little practice; you want them slightly crispy at first bite and meltingly tender in your mouth. The trick for light, airy cookies is to use whipped butter instead of sticks.

YIELDS 60 TO 70 COOKIES

2 cups slivered blanched almonds, toasted until lightly golden

1 pound whipped unsalted sweet cream butter at room temperature

2 egg yolks

½ cup confectioners' sugar plus 3 cups more for dusting

2 teaspoons pure vanilla extract

2 tablespoons cognac

4 to 5 cups all-purpose flour, sifted

Preheat oven to 350 degrees.

Process the almonds in a food processor or high-performance blender, pulsing until they are coarsely ground. They should retain a slight texture, not become a very fine meal. Set aside.

In the bowl of an electric mixer fitted with the paddle attachment, beat together the butter, egg yolks, and ½ cup of the confectioners' sugar on medium-high speed until light and fluffy, about 6 minutes. Reduce speed to low and add the almonds, vanilla extract, and cognac. Increase speed to medium-high and beat for another 2 to 3 minutes, until smooth. Scrape down the sides of the bowl a couple of times during mixing.

Reduce speed to low and add the flour, a little at a time, until the dough comes together and is soft and not sticky. You probably will use about 4½ cups of flour. Remove the dough from the mixer and knead by hand for 1 or 2 minutes to make sure everything is incorporated.

Using a tablespoon as a measure, scoop out small, equal-size pieces of dough, shape them into half-moons, and place them 1 inch apart on 2 large, ungreased cookie sheets. If the dough becomes too warm and difficult to work with, place it in the refrigerator for a few minutes to firm up. Bake for 15 to 20 minutes or until the cookies are a pale yellow gold. (Do not brown.) Remove from oven and cool slightly on the baking sheets, about 5 minutes.

Sift about 1 cup of the remaining confectioners' sugar onto a large sheet of wax paper. Using a small spatula, transfer the warm cookies from the baking sheets to the sugar-coated wax paper. Liberally sift the remaining confectioners' sugar over the top and sides of the cookies so that they are bright white and completely covered with sugar.

Revani *(reh-vah-NEE)*

ALMOND, ORANGE, AND SEMOLINA CAKE

Revani, or *ravani*, is one of my favorite cakes of all time. It is a traditional syrup-soaked Greek cake that is found in various incarnations in cuisines across the eastern Mediterranean region.

SERVES 10 TO 12

FOR THE CAKE

1 cup (2 sticks) unsalted butter, at room temperature

1½ cups granulated sugar

6 large eggs, separated

1 tablespoon Grand Marnier or Cointreau

2 teaspoons orange zest

1 tablespoon freshly squeezed orange juice

1 cup all-purpose flour

1 cup coarse semolina flour

1 tablespoon baking powder

¼ teaspoon sea salt plus 1 pinch

½ cup slivered blanched almonds, lightly toasted and finely chopped

FOR THE SYRUP

2 cups water

2 cups sugar

1 (1-inch wide) slice orange peel, 2 inches long

1 cinnamon stick

Preheat oven to 375 degrees. Butter a 9 × 13-inch baking dish.

In the bowl of an electric mixer fitted with the paddle attachment, beat together the butter and sugar on medium-high speed until light and fluffy, about 3 minutes. With the mixer running on low speed, add the egg yolks, 1 at a time, mixing until well combined. Then add the Grand Marnier or Cointreau, orange zest, and orange juice, mixing for 1 minute more. Scrape down the sides of the bowl twice during mixing.

In another mixing bowl, whisk together the all-purpose flour, semolina flour, baking powder, and ¼ teaspoon of the salt, then stir in the almonds. With the motor running on low speed, slowly add the flour-almond mixture, one-third at a time, to the batter. Mix only until just combined. Transfer the batter to a large mixing bowl, and set aside. Wash and dry the bowl of the electric mixer very well, making sure there is no grease left inside the bowl.

Fit the mixer with the whisk attachment and beat the egg whites together with the remaining pinch of salt until stiff peaks form, about 3 to 5 minutes. Gently fold a large spoonful of the egg whites into the almond batter to lighten the batter. Then add the lightened batter back into the egg whites, very gently folding them together until just combined. You do not want to lose any of the airy volume from the egg whites.

Transfer the batter to the prepared pan, using an offset spatula to smooth the top into an even layer. Place the pan in the preheated oven and bake for 25 to 30 minutes or until golden brown and a cake tester or toothpick inserted in the center of the cake comes out clean.

While the cake is baking, combine all of the syrup ingredients in a medium, nonreactive saucepan. Bring to a boil over medium-high heat, reduce heat to medium, and simmer for 15 minutes, until it resembles a light maple syrup. Cool slightly, then carefully remove and discard the orange peel and cinnamon stick. Set the syrup aside.

When the cake is done, immediately pour the hot syrup over the top. Cover with foil and let the cake sit at room temperature for at least 1 hour to cool and absorb the syrup. Slice into pieces, and serve. *Revani* will keep, covered tightly, at room temperature for up to 4 days.

Tourta *(TOOR-tah)*

AUNT APHRODITE'S SOUR CHERRY SUMMER DESSERT

My aunt Aphrodite (her nickname is Rula) made this no-cook dessert for our family every summer when we were growing up. She was very proud of her homemade sour cherry preserves, which were delicious! If you search your local gourmet store, you usually can find sour cherry preserves, which will work perfectly in this recipe.

YIELDS 24 PIECES

2 cups heavy whipping cream

1 cup confectioners' sugar

2 cups fat-free Greek yogurt

2 packages Papadopoulos Petit Beurre cookies (or other sweet, flat butter cookies) (about 65 to 70 cookies)

2½ cups homemade or gourmet sour cherry preserves

In the bowl of an electric mixer fitted with the whisk attachment, beat the whipping cream to stiff peaks. Add the confectioners' sugar and gently fold in the yogurt, being careful not to deflate the whipped cream.

Line the bottom of a 9 × 13-inch baking pan with 1 layer of the cookies. Spread one-third of the cream mixture evenly over the cookies. Add a second layer of cookies, followed by a second layer of the cream mixture. Top with the remaining cookies and the remaining layer of the cream mixture. Refrigerate, uncovered, for 1 hour to set up. Remove from the refrigerator, and spread the sour cherry preserves evenly over the top, gently pressing any whole cherries into the top layer of cream.

Cover the pan and refrigerate overnight.

Slice into 24 pieces and serve.

Rizogalo *(ree-ZOH-ghah-loh)*

RICE PUDDING

Who doesn't love rice pudding? It is a dessert served around the world, in various cultures, in different styles, and with different flavorings. People love it so much that there is a successful rice pudding restaurant in New York City called Rice to Riches, which celebrates the diversity found in this deceptively simple creation. This Greek version has a true custard pudding base, which makes it velvety and creamy. I love it!

SERVES 4 TO 6

2 cups water plus 3 tablespoons, divided
1 cup long-grain white rice
4 cups milk
1½ cups granulated sugar
2 teaspoons cornstarch
2 egg yolks
½ teaspoon pure vanilla powder *or* 1 teaspoon
    pure vanilla extract
1 teaspoon ground cinnamon, *or* to taste

Combine 2 cups of the water and the rice in a medium saucepan set over medium-high heat. As the water begins to simmer, stir in the milk, and reduce heat to medium. Bring back to a boil, watching very carefully so that the milk does not boil over. Immediately reduce heat to medium-low and simmer, uncovered, until the mixture thickens, about 15 minutes. Add the sugar and stir to combine. Reduce heat to low.

Meanwhile, in a medium mixing bowl, dilute the cornstarch in the remaining 3 tablespoons of water. Whisk in the egg yolks along with the vanilla powder or extract. Slowly add about 1 cup of the hot rice mixture to the egg yolk mixture to temper the eggs, stirring vigorously. Then slowly return the tempered egg yolk mixture back to the rice on the stove, stirring constantly so as not to scramble the eggs. Continue to cook and stir over low heat until the pudding has a smooth, creamy texture, about 3 minutes. Do not allow the mixture to become too thick (like oatmeal) because it will continue to thicken as it cools. Remove from heat, and transfer to individual serving bowls.

Sprinkle each serving with a little of the ground cinnamon, to taste, and serve warm.

———————— ≡ ————————

DEBBIE'S TIP: Cold rice pudding has a consistency close to that of flan, so if you love flan, you'll enjoy cold *Rizogalo*. To serve it cold, refrigerate the rice pudding for at least 3 hours or overnight.

Koulourakia *(koo-loo-RAH-kee-ah)*

TRADITIONAL GREEK COOKIES

Koulourakia are as Greek as chocolate chip cookies are American. They are found in every bakery across Greece, often proudly displayed in the window. When you enter a Greek bakery, the proprietors frequently offer a *koulouraki* (or ten) on the house as a means of saying thank you for coming in. It is what we Greeks call *philotimo*.

YIELDS 55 TO 60

1 cup (2 sticks) unsalted butter, at room temperature

½ cup granulated sugar

4 large eggs

½ teaspoon pure vanilla extract

3½ cups all-purpose flour

1 teaspoon baking powder

¼ teaspoon baking soda

¼ teaspoon baker's ammonia (ammonium carbonate) (see tip on page 261)

⅛ teaspoon sea salt

½ teaspoon ground cinnamon

2 to 3 tablespoons sesame seeds (optional)

Preheat oven to 350 degrees. Line 2 large cookie sheets with unbleached parchment paper.

In the bowl of an electric mixer fitted with the paddle attachment, beat together the butter and sugar on medium-high speed until light and fluffy, about 3 minutes. With the motor running on low speed, add 3 of the eggs to the butter mixture, 1 at a time, allowing each to be incor-porated before adding the next. Then add the vanilla, and mix until just combined.

In another large mixing bowl, whisk together the flour, baking powder, baking soda, baker's ammonia (if available), salt, and cinnamon. With the motor of the electric mixer running on low, slowly add the dry mixture to the egg mixture one-third at a time, pausing after each addition. Mix just until the dough no longer sticks to the sides of the bowl, being careful not to over-mix, or your cookies will be tough.

Very lightly oil a marble baking slab or a large plastic cutting board as well as your hands. Using a tablespoon as a measure, scoop out a piece of the dough. Roll the dough between your hands and/or on the oiled surface until it resembles a long Tootsie Roll, about 8½ inches long. Fold in half and twist together 2 to 3 times to form a cookie twist. Press the ends together and lay on the prepared cookie sheet. Repeat with the remaining dough. Keep some paper towels nearby in case your hands or the surface get too greasy.

In a small mixing bowl, lightly beat the remain-ing egg. Using a pastry brush, brush the egg over the top of each cookie. Evenly sprinkle the cookies with the sesame seeds (if using), press-ing them very lightly into the dough. Transfer to the oven and bake for 25 to 30 minutes or until

(recipe continues)

golden brown. Remove the cookies, cool for 3 to 4 minutes on the cookie sheets, and transfer to cooling racks to cool completely. *Koulourakia* will keep in an airtight container at room temperature for up to 1 week.

─────── 🇬🇷 ───────

DEBBIE'S TIP: Baker's ammonia is a European baking leavening agent that is used quite often in traditional Greek baking. It yields an incredible crispness that other leavening agents can't duplicate. You can typically find it online or in Mediterranean or Greek specialty markets, or in Scandinavian markets under the name "hartshorn." You may notice a smell of ammonia when using baker's ammonia. This is normal, and the gas cooks out. If you cannot find baker's ammonia, increase the baking soda to ½ teaspoon (instead of ¼ teaspoon).

VEGAN VARIATION

1 cup vegetable oil
¾ cup granulated sugar
1 cup freshly squeezed orange juice
¼ teaspoon pure vanilla extract
3½ to 4 cups all-purpose flour
1½ teaspoons baking powder
¼ teaspoon baking soda
¼ teaspoon baker's ammonia (ammonium carbonate) (see tip)
⅛ teaspoon sea salt
½ teaspoon ground cinnamon
2 tablespoons sesame seeds

In the bowl of an electric mixer fitted with the paddle attachment, beat together the oil and sugar on medium-high speed until light and fluffy, about 2 to 3 minutes. With the motor running on low, add the orange juice. Then add the vanilla and mix until just combined.

In another large mixing bowl, whisk together 3½ cups of the flour, baking powder, baking soda, baker's ammonia (if available), salt, and cinnamon. With the motor of the electric mixer running on low, slowly add the dry mixture to the wet mixture one-third at a time, pausing after each addition. Mix just until the dough no longer sticks to the sides of the bowl, being careful not to over-mix, or your cookies will be tough. If your dough is still wet and sticky, add the remaining flour slowly, 1 tablespoon at a time, until the dough no longer sticks to the sides of the bowl.

Omit egg step and continue with the procedure for the nonvegan *Koulourakia.*

Paksimathia *(pahk-see-MAH-thee-ah)*

GREEK BISCOTTI

This is a Greek version of the Italian biscotti. In recent years, bakers have made several variations by adding raisins, chocolate chips, walnuts, and pistachios, but I am partial to Mom's old fashioned recipe, which uses almonds.

YIELDS 60 TO 65

1 cup vegetable oil
¾ cup granulated sugar
4 large eggs
½ teaspoon pure vanilla extract
3½ cups flour
1½ teaspoons baking powder
½ teaspoon baking soda
¼ teaspoon sea salt
¾ cups finely chopped raw unsalted almonds (a high-performance blender or food processor works well)

Preheat oven to 350 degrees. Line 2 large cookie sheets with unbleached parchment paper.

In the bowl of an electric mixer fitted with the paddle attachment, beat together the oil and sugar on medium-high speed until light and fluffy, about 2 to 3 minutes. With the motor running, add the eggs, 1 at a time, allowing each to be incorporated before adding the next. Then add the vanilla and mix until just combined.

In another large mixing bowl, whisk together the flour, baking powder, baking soda, and salt. With the motor of the electric mixer running on low, slowly add the dry mixture to the wet mixture one-third at a time, pausing after each addition. Mix just until the dough no longer sticks to the sides of the bowl, being careful not to over-mix, or your cookies will be tough. Remove the bowl from the mixer and work the almonds into the dough by hand.

Very lightly oil a marble baking slab or a large plastic cutting board as well as your hands, and lightly oil a large serving spoon to use as a measure. Scoop out a heaping portion of the dough with the oiled serving spoon and shape into the form of a long pretzel roll or a small baguette, about 9 inches long. Continue with the remaining dough. You should end up with 5 (9 × 3-inch) logs of dough. Keep some paper towels nearby in case your hands or the surface gets too greasy. Transfer the dough logs to the prepared cookie sheets, taking care not to place them too close together, as they will expand in the oven.

Transfer to preheated oven and bake for 20 to 25 minutes, until lightly browned. Remove from oven, cool for a few minutes until cool enough to handle, and, using a serrated knife, cut each log into ¾-inch slices on a slight diagonal angle. Lay the slices cut side down on the same baking sheets, and return them to the oven to crisp up for another 15 to 20 minutes, or until golden. *Paksimathia* will keep in an airtight container at room temperature for up to 1 week.

VEGAN VARIATION

1 cup vegetable oil

¾ cup granulated sugar

1 cup orange juice

½ teaspoon pure vanilla extract

3½ cups flour

2 teaspoons baking powder

½ teaspoon baking soda

¼ teaspoon sea salt

1 teaspoon ground cinnamon

¾ cups finely chopped raw unsalted almonds (a high-performance blender or food processor works well)

In the bowl of an electric mixer fitted with the paddle attachment, beat together the oil and sugar on medium-high speed until light and fluffy, about 2 to 3 minutes. With the motor running on low, add the orange juice. Then add the vanilla and mix until just combined.

In another large mixing bowl, whisk together the flour, baking powder, baking soda, salt, and cinnamon. With the motor of the electric mixer running on low, slowly add the dry mixture to the wet mixture one-third at a time, pausing after each addition. Mix just until the dough no longer sticks to the sides of the bowl, being careful not to over-mix, or your cookies will be tough.

Continue with the procedure for the nonvegan *Paksimathia*.

Galaktoboureko *(ghah-lah-KTOH-boo-ree-koh)*

CLASSIC PHYLLO CUSTARD PIE

This dessert was always a favorite in my neighborhood growing up. My friends from school would come over regularly and beg my sweet mom to make it for them. Although the recipe may appear difficult to master, it is quite easy to make. The most difficult parts are trimming the top layers of phyllo dough to fit the pan and scoring the top before baking. A little patience with the final steps yields one of the most delectable Greek pastries of all time!

YIELDS 16 TO 20 PIECES

FOR THE PIE

6 cups milk

1 cup fine semolina flour

¼ teaspoon pure vanilla extract

5 large eggs

1 cup granulated sugar

2 tablespoons unsalted butter at room
    temperature

1 (1-pound) package phyllo dough sheets
    (13 × 18 inches), thawed (see tip, page 112)

½ cup (1 stick) unsalted butter, melted

FOR THE SYRUP

2½ cups granulated sugar

1½ cups water

1 (1-inch-wide) slice lemon peel, 2 inches long

1 teaspoon freshly squeezed lemon juice (1 lemon)

Preheat oven to 350 degrees. Grease a 9 × 13-inch baking dish.

In a medium saucepan, bring the milk to a simmer over medium-high heat, watching closely so that it does not boil over. Slowly stir in the semolina and keep stirring until the mixture thickens. Stir in the vanilla, cook for 1 minute more, and remove from heat.

In a medium mixing bowl, whisk the eggs together with the sugar until well combined. To temper the eggs, slowly add about 1 cup of the semolina mixture to the egg mixture, whisking vigorously to avoid scrambling the eggs. When well mixed, slowly add the tempered egg mixture back into the hot semolina mixture, again stirring vigorously to avoid scrambling the eggs. Add the room-temperature butter and stir so it is evenly incorporated. Set the custard aside, but stir every so often so that a skin does not develop on top.

Roll the phyllo dough out on a flat surface, working quickly and keeping it covered to prevent it from drying out. Place 1 phyllo sheet into the baking dish at a time, centering it in the pan and letting the edges hang over the sides. Brush each sheet of phyllo with a little of the melted butter, but do not brush the overhanging edges. Continue in this manner until you have used 9 phyllo dough sheets. Spread the custard evenly over the 9 layers of phyllo dough. Fold the overhanging phyllo dough over the filling, then continue to layer the phyllo dough on top, again brushing each sheet with the melted butter, until you have used all of the dough. Trim the top layers of phyllo to fit the baking dish. Brush the top liberally with the melted butter, taking care to seal the top layers closed with it. Sprinkle the top very lightly with about a tablespoon of water.

With a very sharp knife, score the top 4 layers of the phyllo into 16 to 20 pieces, taking care not to cut all the way through into the custard. Bake, uncovered, for 55 to 60 minutes or until flaky and golden brown.

While the *galaktoboureko* is baking, make the syrup. In a medium, nonreactive saucepan, stir the sugar and water together, and add the lemon peel. Set over medium-high heat, bring to a boil, and cook for 5 minutes. Skim off any foam that floats to the top. After 5 minutes, stir in the lemon juice, and cook for 1 minute more. Remove from heat, allow to cool to room temperature, and remove the lemon peel.

When the *galaktoboureko* comes out of the oven, immediately ladle the room-temperature syrup over the top. Cool for 45 minutes and then cut all the way through. *Galaktoboureko* is best served slightly warm.

Trigona Thessalonikis *(TREE-ghoh-nah theh-sah-loh-NEE-kees)*

ALMOND CUSTARD TRIANGLES

Be warned! If you like almonds, you will forever crave these custardy confections after just one bite. This dessert originates in the city of Thessaloniki, the second largest city in Greece, for which they are named. Thessaloniki is a big college town located about 2½ hours from the village where my family is from. It was always fun for us kids to escape for a weekend to the big city.

YIELDS 25 TRIANGLES

10 tablespoons butter (1¼ sticks), melted
5¼ cups blanched slivered almonds
3⅓ cups water
3¼ cups granulated sugar
2 large eggs, beaten
1 teaspoon pure vanilla extract
1½ pounds phyllo dough (1½ packages;
    13 × 18 inches), thawed
½ cup confectioners' sugar (optional)

Preheat oven to 350 degrees. Brush a large baking pan or cookie sheet with some of the melted butter.

In a food processor or high-performance blender, grind the almonds into a fine meal and set aside.

Set a medium saucepan over medium heat and add the water and sugar. Bring to a boil, stirring constantly, then reduce heat to medium-low, and cook for 10 to 12 minutes, until the sugar is dissolved and the syrup is smooth. Stir in the ground almonds, increase heat to medium, and bring to a boil again just to cook the almonds. Once the mixture boils, remove the saucepan from heat and set aside to cool. Once the almond mixture has cooled completely, stir in the eggs and the vanilla.

Roll the phyllo dough out on a flat surface, working quickly and keeping it covered to prevent it from drying out. Cut the phyllo lengthwise into 6- to 8-inch strips. Cover the unused phyllo with wax paper and a clean kitchen towel. Lay 2 phyllo strips on top of each other and brush the top with melted butter. Place 1 tablespoon of the almond custard on the bottom corner of phyllo strip, and fold up into a triangle, as if folding the American flag. Brush both sides of the folded triangle with melted butter and place on the prepared baking sheet. Continue in this manner until you have used up all the custard.

Place the baking sheet in the preheated oven, and bake for 30 to 35 minutes or until golden brown. Remove from oven, let cool, and dust with the confectioners' sugar, if desired.

Ta Ipolipa
THE EXTRAS

I want to share a few staples in my life with my readers. Whether it's a quick breakfast on the go or some delicious homemade bread and preserves, these are recipes that I just can't live without. Although they do not fit in any of the other categories, I thought they deserved a category of their own!

Summertime Breakfast Medley

Growing up, I spent many summers with my grandmother in Greece. Her favorite breakfast was beautiful ripe, red watermelon served ice cold with feta and fresh, homemade bread. Soon after she introduced me to it, this unconventional breakfast became my favorite too. Today, my life moves a little faster than it did when I used to sit with my yiayia in the olive groves watching the birds go by, so over the years I have adapted this breakfast to fit an on-the-go lifestyle.

SERVES 4

4 (¼-inch) slices brine-packed Greek feta
4 thick slices *Uncle Dimitri's Homemade Bread*
   (page 277) *or* other bakery-fresh bread
2 teaspoons extra-virgin olive oil
¼ teaspoon dried oregano
Freshly ground black pepper, to taste
4 large leaves fresh basil
4 thick slices fresh, ripe watermelon

Put 1 slice of feta on top of each slice of bread. Drizzle with a little olive oil, followed by a sprinkle of the dried oregano and a couple of grinds of pepper. Top each sandwich with 1 basil leaf and a slice of watermelon.

Enjoy with a small cup of Greek coffee.

Debbie's Breakfast Smoothie

I have been drinking this smoothie for breakfast since I was a teenager. One morning, I just grabbed the first things I saw when I opened the refrigerator and blended them up. Simple, basic, delicious, and nutritious, it is such a refreshing start to the day.

SERVES 2

2 cups plain Greek yogurt
2 tablespoons honey
¼ teaspoon cinnamon
6 to 8 fresh figs *or* your favorite fruit, fresh in season or frozen
10 to 15 walnut halves
½ cup ice
Skim or nondairy milk *or* water, as needed

Place the yogurt, honey, cinnamon, figs or other fruit, walnuts, and ice in a blender, and blend on high to combine. With the motor running, slowly add the milk or water until desired consistency is reached.

Pour into tall glasses, and enjoy.

Savory Summer Fruit Salad

Traditionally, this is something my family would eat for breakfast. But you can certainly serve it any time of the day . . . I love it for a midnight snack!

SERVES 4

3 to 4 cups ripe watermelon, cut into 2-inch cubes
2 fresh, ripe peaches, halved, pitted, and thinly sliced
½ pound brine-packed Greek feta, drained and crumbled
½ seedless English cucumber, peeled and diced
2 tablespoons chiffonade-cut fresh mint leaves
2 to 3 tablespoons honey, to taste

Combine all of the ingredients except the honey in a large salad bowl. Drizzle the honey over the top, toss together, and serve immediately.

————— 🇬🇷 —————

YIAYIA'S TIP: It's easy to make a chiffonade cut of fresh herbs. Chiffonade looks pretty, and the herbs will retain their color without bruising or blackening. Simply stack the leaves, roll them up like a cigar, and use a sharp knife to make thin, crosswise cuts. You'll be left with beautiful ribbons of herbs.

Easy Baked Croutons

These easy and delicious croutons will lend crunch and pizzazz to your favorite soups and salads. Try this recipe with any kind of bread you and your family enjoy, such as herb or olive oil. Add a little garlic powder (which won't burn in the oven like fresh garlic can) for additional flavor.

YIELDS 7 TO 8 CUPS

1 loaf day-old country bread (about 1 pound)
3 tablespoons extra-virgin olive oil
½ teaspoon sea salt
¼ teaspoon freshly ground black pepper
¼ teaspoon garlic powder (optional)

Preheat oven to 350 degrees. Line a large baking sheet with unbleached parchment paper.

Trim the ends off the bread and cut the loaf into ½-inch slices. Cut each slice into 1-inch squares, and transfer to the baking sheet. Toss the croutons with the olive oil, salt, pepper, and garlic powder (if using). Bake for 12 to 15 minutes, stirring the croutons halfway through, or until toasted golden brown on all sides. Remove from oven and let cool.

—————— ▤ ——————

DEBBIE'S TIP: *Uncle Dimitri's Homemade Bread (page 277) makes especially delicious croutons.*

Bougatsa *(boo-GHAH-tsah)*

Bougatsa is, in my opinion, the Greek version of a cream puff. It is traditionally made with layers of phyllo dough and a custard filling. This staple in Greek households is relatively simple to assemble. Try it for a special-occasion breakfast!

SERVES 8 TO 10

4 cups milk

1 cup granulated sugar

1 tablespoon finely grated lemon zest (1 lemon)

¾ cup fine semolina flour

2 large eggs

½ teaspoon pure vanilla extract

1 (1-pound) package phyllo dough sheets
  (13 × 18 inches), thawed (see tip, page 112)

½ cup (1 stick) unsalted butter, melted

3 tablespoons ground cinnamon

3 tablespoons confectioners' sugar

With a wooden spoon, stir together the milk, sugar, and lemon zest in a medium saucepan set over medium heat. When bubbles appear around the edges but before the mixture boils, add the semolina flour very slowly, stirring vigorously to combine. Keep stirring until the semolina flour cooks and the mixture thickens, about 3 minutes. Remove from heat.

Quickly whisk the eggs and vanilla together in a medium mixing bowl. Slowly add about 1 cup of the hot milk mixture to temper the eggs (see tip, page 70), whisking constantly to combine. When well combined, slowly add the egg mixture back into the hot milk and flour mixture, stirring vigorously to avoid scrambling the eggs. Set the saucepan over low heat, stirring constantly to prevent lumps, and cook for 1 or 2 minutes more to create a smooth custard. Remove from heat, and set aside.

Preheat oven to 350 degrees. Butter a 9 × 13-inch baking dish.

Roll the phyllo dough out on a flat surface, working quickly and keeping it covered to prevent it from drying out. To assemble the *bougatsa*, lay 1 sheet of the phyllo dough in the bottom of the baking dish, offsetting it slightly from the center toward the top left corner. Using a large pastry brush, brush the phyllo dough lightly with the melted butter, leaving the overhang dry. Working very quickly, repeat this process in the upper right corner, the lower right corner, and the lower left corner. Start again in the upper left corner, and repeat, so that you end up with 8 sheets of buttered phyllo with an overhanging edge all the way around the baking dish. Lay 2 more sheets of phyllo dough in the center of the pan, brushing each one with butter and letting each hang over the sides as well.

Pour all of the custard into the center of the phyllo sheets in the baking dish and sprinkle 1 tablespoon of the cinnamon evenly over the custard. Then, layer the remaining 8 sheets of phyllo, 1 at a time, on top of the custard and in the center of the baking dish, brushing each sheet with the melted butter. Trim the edges of top 8 sheets to fit the baking dish. Fold the overhanging edges of the lower layers of phyllo over the top layers, sealing in the custard and enclosing the *bougatsa*.

Brush the top liberally with melted butter, being sure to seal the edges closed. Transfer the *bou-gatsa* to the preheated oven and bake, uncovered, for 50 to 60 minutes or until flaky and golden brown.

Mix the remaining 2 tablespoons of cinnamon together with the confectioners' sugar. Remove the *bougatsa* from the oven, and, while very hot, sprinkle the cinnamon-sugar mixture over the top. Serve warm or at room temperature.

Uncle Dimitri's Homemade Bread

My uncle Dimitri literally grew up in a bakery. His grandfather owned the bakery, passed it down to his father, and then his father passed it on to him. Anytime I've ever needed a baked goods recipe, Dimitri was the man I called. He also happens to be a licensed electrician, which has certainly proved useful through the years when dealing with temperamental ovens. This bread is easy, foolproof, and delicious. One of my favorite things to do as kid was to slice off the end of a cooling loaf and scoop out the inside, warm, yummy doughy part. I'd slather it with butter, scarf it down, and replace the end. Then my family would slice into a hollow loaf and know that I'd struck again!

YIELDS 2 LOAVES

2 cups warm water (110 degrees, see tip, page 278)
2 packages (4½ teaspoons) active dry yeast
2 tablespoons plus 2 teaspoons honey, divided
6 cups all-purpose flour, plus more as needed
1 tablespoon sea salt
4 tablespoons extra-virgin olive oil, plus more as needed

Lightly oil a large wooden or plastic mixing bowl.

Add ½ cup of the water to a medium mixing bowl. Add the yeast and 2 teaspoons of the honey, and whisk until combined. Let the yeast dissolve for about 5 minutes, until it is frothy.

In a large mixing bowl, whisk together the flour and the salt, and set aside.

Transfer the yeast mixture to the warmed bowl of an electric mixer fitted with the dough hook. Add the remaining 1½ cups water, 4 tablespoons of olive oil, and the remaining 2 tablespoons of honey. Give the mixture a quick stir by hand to combine. Then add 3 cups of the flour-salt mixture. Set the bowl onto the mixer and mix on low speed until the flour mixture comes together, about 2 minutes. Add the remaining 3 cups of the flour-salt mixture and mix on medium-low speed until the dough comes away from the sides of the bowl and begins to creep up the dough hook, about 2 to 3 minutes.

Transfer the dough to a lightly floured surface and flour your hands. Knead the dough by hand for 3 to 5 minutes, until it is very smooth and elastic and almost does not stick to your hands. Shape the dough into a ball, and place in the oiled mixing bowl, turning once to oil the top of the dough. Cover with plastic wrap and then with a towel or a blanket, and set in a warm, draft-free place for 1 to 2 hours, or until it has doubled in size. You will know it is ready when the dough does not spring back to its original shape after you push your finger into it.

Lightly oil 2 9 × 5-inch loaf pans and keep them in a warm place. When dough has risen, transfer

(recipe continues)

it to a large plastic or wooden cutting board, punch it down with the heel of your hand to flatten, and cut in half. Press and shape each half of the dough into a 9-inch-long rectangle, about ½-inch thick. Fold the rectangles in half long ways, overlapping the edges slightly in the middle and pinching the seam closed. Transfer the folded dough, seam side down, to the prepared pans, and cover loosely with a blanket or a towel.

Alternatively, knead each half of the dough again for about 1 minute and shape each half into a round loaf. Place the loaves a good distance apart on a warmed (not hot, not cold) large, well-oiled baking sheet or on 2 separate baking sheets. If the sheet is too cold, the dough will fall. Cover each loaf loosely again with a clean dishtowel or blanket.

Set the pans or the baking sheet aside again in a warm, draft-free place to rise until doubled in volume, about 45 to 60 minutes more.

Preheat oven to 400 degrees. Brush the tops of the loaves with olive oil. Place the loaf pans or baking sheet into the oven and bake until golden and the loaves sound hollow when tapped, about 30 minutes. Remove from oven, lifting loaves from baking sheets with a large spatula. Turn loaves out of pans onto clean dishtowels or a cooling rack to cool for 30 minutes.

Slice and serve.

DEBBIE'S TIP: It is very important that mixing bowls and baking pans are warmed and not cold; otherwise, the yeast will take many hours to rise. Also, I find it is very useful to use an instant-read or candy thermometer to make sure the water I'm using is always at 110 degrees. Water that is too hot will kill the yeast, while water that is too cold will slow its growth.

Dessert Fruit Salad

Sometimes I want something for dessert but do not want to go through a big production for something refreshing and a little sweet. This quick, healthy dessert hits the spot, especially after a rich meal. This is more along the lines of what would traditionally be served after a big meal in Greece—a big bowl of refreshing, fresh fruit for all to enjoy.

SERVES 6

2 cups cubed honeydew melon

2 cups cubed watermelon

2 cups cherries, pitted

2 large peaches *or* 2 Granny Smith (or other tart apple), thinly sliced

1 tablespoon finely chopped fresh mint plus 6 leaves for garnish

2 tablespoons freshly squeezed lemon juice (1 lemon)

2 tablespoons honey *or* maple syrup

Pinch of sea salt

1½ cups Greek yogurt (optional)

In a large mixing bowl, gently toss together the melons, cherries, peaches or apples, and chopped mint. In a small bowl, whisk together the lemon juice, honey or maple syrup, and salt. Drizzle the dressing over the fruit and gently stir to combine.

Let stand at room temperature for 5 minutes and serve, topping each serving with a ¼-cup dollop of the yogurt, if desired. Set 1 mint leaf on top of the yogurt as garnish.

DEBBIE'S TIP: It may seem odd to add a pinch of sea salt to fruit, but actually it is a great trick to maximize the flavor of the fruit. The salt not only brings out the intense fruit flavors but entices them to release their juices, which is awesome for a treat like this. Yum!

Aunt Malama's Peach Preserves

When I was five years old, I loved to pick fresh peaches in my aunt Malama's yard in Naoussa, Greece. The peaches were so sweet and juicy that when I took one bite, the juice would run all the way down my arm. I remember thinking those peaches were massive—the size of watermelons! When you are five, everything seems gigantic. However, the one thing that isn't exaggerated is just how delicious Malama's homemade peach preserves truly are. She has graciously shared her recipe with me so that everyone can *can* . . . and I don't mean dance!

This easy, three-ingredient recipe must be cooked slowly for 30 minutes, which seems like a long time, but that is how the immense peach flavor and dark orangey-caramel color is developed. The longer cooking time also thickens the preserves without store-bought pectin or gelling agents. Choose organic (vegan) sugar, if available, for richer flavor. Enjoy this pure, simple, delicious treat on toast, spooned over a slice of cake, or straight from the jar! You can also add it to plain Greek yogurt for a fabulous breakfast treat or a snack.

YIELDS 8½ CUPS

5 pounds ripe peaches, peeled (see tip, page 282), pitted, and sliced
8 cups organic vegan cane sugar
2 tablespoons freshly squeezed lemon juice (1 lemon)

Toss the peaches together with the sugar in a large stockpot using a large spatula or impeccably clean hands. Crush the mixture with your hands or a potato masher until the peaches break down and release their juice and the sugar begins to dissolve. Stir in the lemon juice and set the pot over medium-high heat. Bring to a boil, reduce heat to medium, and stir constantly for 30 minutes. A layer of foam will develop on the top but then slowly dissolve back into the preserves as they cook down and thicken. Do not leave the pot unattended and do not stop stirring, or the sugar will stick to the bottom and burn.

After 30 minutes, when the preserves begin to really firm up, scoop 2 to 3 tablespoons into a small, heatproof dish, and put it in the freezer for 3 minutes. The preserves will thicken considerably as they cool. Judge the final consistency by pushing the chilled preserves with your

(recipe continues)

finger—if they "wrinkle," the preserves have set. If you desire thicker preserves, cook a few minutes longer and test again.

If serving immediately, pour the preserves into a bowl and cool to room temperature, or refrigerate, tightly covered, for up to 3 weeks. If canning for shelf-stable storage, follow the directions from the manufacturer of your canning system.

———————— 🇬🇷 ————————

DEBBIE'S TIP: Aunt Malama taught me an easy trick for peeling peaches. Drop them into boiling water for 60 seconds, remove them with a slotted spoon, and dunk them into a large bowl of ice water to stop the cooking. The skins should slip off easily. If your peaches are not quite ripe, you may need to boil them a little longer.

Tsoureki *(tsoo-REH-kee)*

GREEK EASTER BREAD

Every Easter, my mom makes a gazillion loaves of *tsourekia* for us to enjoy and to give away to friends and family. The Easter Lenten season is one of my mom's favorite times of year because she can share this bread, which she makes with so much love, with those she cares about. With my mom's heart and spirit in mind, this recipe yields 7 to 8 loaves so that you, too, can give them away to those you love.

YIELDS 7 TO 8 LOAVES

9½ cups all-purpose flour

3 packages (6¾ teaspoons) active dry yeast

½ cup warm water (110 degrees, see tip, page 278)

2 cups milk

1 cup (2 sticks) unsalted butter at room temperature

1½ cups granulated sugar

¼ teaspoon sea salt

5 large eggs

¼ teaspoon room-temperature water

1 tablespoon sesame seeds *or* 4 to 6 tablespoons sliced almonds (optional)

Sift the flour into a very large wooden or plastic salad bowl. Make a small well in the center of the flour. Dissolve the yeast in the warm water, and slowly pour the yeast mixture into the well in the flour. With a small spoon, mix a little bit of the flour into the yeast and water mixture, but keep the yeast mixture liquid and not too thick.

Cover the bowl with a kitchen towel and set it in a warm place for 20 minutes.

Heat the milk in a medium saucepan set over medium heat until it just begins to boil. Remove from heat and add the butter, sugar, and salt. Allow the butter to melt and stir together to combine the mixture. Set aside to cool slightly.

After the flour and yeast mixture has sat covered for 20 minutes, beat together 4 of the eggs. Remove the towel from the bowl. Very slowly pour half of the warm milk mixture around the edges of the bowl, stirring the flour into the milk mixture with a wooden spoon. Begin to incorporate the yeast as you stir. Then stir half of the beaten eggs into the flour mixture in the same manner. Follow with the remaining milk, then with the remaining beaten eggs. Once everything has just come together, begin to knead the dough in the bowl. It will be very sticky at first, but as you work the dough, it will come together and stop sticking to your hands. Knead the dough for 13 to 15 minutes, until it becomes smooth and soft and no longer sticks to your fingers or the sides of the bowl.

Put the entire bowl into a large plastic bag. Cover the bowl with a large towel or a small blanket, and set it in a warm place, away from any air conditioning or drafts. My mom actually used to

(continued)

set it on the sofa in the living room—where, by the way, we were never allowed as children! Let the dough rise for 1 hour.

After 1 hour, remove the dough from the bag. Set out a large wooden cutting board to assemble the loaves. Warm up 2 large cookie sheets by running them under very warm water. Dry them well, and line them with unbleached parchment paper.

Pull a softball-size piece of dough from the bowl, cut it, and put it on the cutting board. Cut the small piece of dough into 3 even pieces. Using your hands, roll the 3 pieces of dough into 3 even logs, each 1 foot in length. If the dough gets too sticky, coat your hands with a little olive oil. Braid the 3 logs together, all the way to the end, and gently pinch the ends together to form loaves. Repeat this braiding process with the remaining dough. Transfer the braided dough to the prepared cookie sheets. Put each baking sheet into its own plastic bag, cover with a towel or blanket, and set aside in a warm place for the dough to rise again for 1 hour.

Preheat oven to 350 degrees.

After the loaves have risen, remove the cookie sheets from the bags. Beat the remaining egg with the ¼ teaspoon of water to create an egg wash. Using a large pastry brush, brush each loaf evenly with the egg wash, then sprinkle each loaf evenly with the sesame seeds or sliced almonds. Put the cookie sheets in the preheated oven. Bake until the tops are richly golden and the loaves sound hollow when tapped, about 35 to 40 minutes. Watch closely for the last couple of minutes.

Remove from the oven and immediately transfer the loaves to kitchen or paper towels on the counter to cool. When the loaves are cool, you can serve the bread right away or put the loaves into decorative plastic bags to give as gifts.

Acknowledgments

As I sit down to write these acknowledgments I find myself incredibly overwhelmed with emotion. Where on earth do I begin? How can I possibly thank everyone in my life that has been instrumental in making this idea a reality? In these next pages I will try my very best to express my gratitude to all of you. But more importantly, I hope I will be able to continue to *show* you my gratitude through our relationships on a daily basis.

First and foremost, to my mother Efrosini (Froso) Matenopoulos and my father Niko Matenopoulos. If it were not for their insistence on raising me and my siblings to respect our culture and continue the Greek traditions, this book would not have been possible. Mom and Dad, you showed me unconditional love (even when I sometimes probably didn't deserve it), you raised me to understand the importance of family, you showed me by example to be kind and generous to everyone I meet, and you helped me to always have an open heart. You taught me to always be grateful for life. There are no words in the English or Greek language for that matter to express my gratitude to you, Mama and Baba. Baba, I miss you every day. I wish you were here physically to experience this with us, but I know you are with us every day in spirit to guide and protect us. My love for you is immeasurable. I promise to live by the lessons you have taught me and to always still make you proud. Thank you, Mama, for working so tirelessly on this

book with me. You cooked and styled nearly every dish yourself, and you did a fantastic job. I'm so fortunate to have you as a mother. I love you.

To my sister Maria, her husband Kevin, and their kids Mary-Frances, Niko, and Gabriella. My brother Ike, his wife Tina, and their kids Dimitri and Sophia. Thank you for always sticking by each other through thick and thin and for always making our big loud crazy family so much fun. Thank you all for always being there for me. Maria, thank you for taking endless phone calls from me at all hours of the day to talk me through family recipes. Mary-Frances, thank you for being our production assistant in Greece and agreeing to be on the cover. Thank you for always being my biggest cheerleader.

My best friend since second grade, Ann Theofanos, thank you for always being there for me. It's been quite a journey. I love you, my bestie!

To my other besties Julie Cooper and Susan Ryan. Thank you for always opening your home to me in New York City and always making me feel at home.

To my aunt Aphrodite, Uncle Theothoro, and cousins Aris and Avgerinos, thank you for opening your homes and your hearts, cooking, coordinating shoots, hosting Peter, Jon, and I and always with smiles on your faces and love in your hearts. I'm so fortunate you are my family. To all of your friends in Xanthi, Greece, Ari, who made this book so special by sharing themselves and their knowledge. They made it 1,000 percent better than it would have been. To Yianni (The President), for organizing the indoor farmers' market and the sheep farm shoots and for agreeing to be on the cover as well. Giorgos Mpatzakidis for hosting us at the farmers' market, Apostolos Papadopoulos for showing us around his fresh meat market, Pantelis Pyrgelis for letting us shoot at his sheep farm, Christos Mixalakidis at Fanarakia Restaurant for staying open for us at all hours and treating us to such great meals.

To Peter Capozzi, my partner in this undertaking, my producer, my friend for life. This could *not* have happened without you. I truly mean that. Thank you for the tireless hours and late nights and editing and re-editing and the testing of recipes and the laughter and the tears. We started this journey as friends. We have become family. Thank you for believing in me when I was having a hard time doing so. Thank you for giving me a kick in the butt. Thank you for the honesty and the (sometimes) tough love. We did it Peter!! We did it!! To your family. Your sister Meghan Capozzi Rowe, who took some beautiful additional photos for us, your brother-in-law chef Keith Rowe, who tirelessly shared his culinary knowledge and advice with us, and your parents LaDonna and John for putting up with us and helping test recipes and style the food for some of the photos for the book. We love you!

To Jonathan Falcone, also my partner in this book and friend for life. I have never seen someone work harder and longer and never run out of steam. Without your tenacity, tireless work, and talent this book could have never happened, either. It would have never been a reality. Your ideas and attention to detail are next-to-none, and I feel honored to have worked with you on our first book together. You took plates of food and turned them into beautiful works of art. The gorgeous lifestyle photos you took throughout Greece rival those of famous photographers twice your age and with twice the experience. You are a force to be reckoned with. I also feel honored to call you my friend. Thank you for all the edits and re-edits and your endless hours of work behind the camera, not always in the most ideal situations, as well as in front of the computer. Thank you for trusting me enough and believing in me and the project enough to be a part of it. I truly hope this is just the first of many books we work on together. You're stuck with me for life.

To Yianni (John) Retsios who hosted us in Athens, without you we literally could not have done it. Thank you for wearing so many hats. Producer, tour guide, manager, chauffeur, travel agent, and occasional legal counsel! You are a one-man concierge service. Thank you for doing it all with a smile on your face and a joking lightheartedness. Four words for you: "detained at the Acropolis." To your parents, George and

Theodora Retsios, who trusted us to stay in their home without ever having met us. To your aunt, Lemonia Xepapadakos, who cooked for us every night when we returned to your home, and your uncle, Charalambos Christofilakis, who collected us from the airport. To George Psipsikas, the "Johnny Depp of Greece." Thank you for all of your *philoxenia*.

To Trish Sebben-Krupka, our fantastic editor. Thank you for your tireless work on this book, your recipe testing and advice, your late nights, and your unwavering dedication. Your patience and organization made this work possible, and we could not have completed this book without you.

To Glenn Yeffeth, our publisher at BenBella Books. What can I say? Your vision and belief in this book since day one has been both an honor and an inspiration. Thank you for taking a chance on a first-time cookbook writer and for introducing us to the brilliant Dr. Michael Ozner. This project means the world to me, and both Peter and I could not be more grateful to you. This is just the beginning!

To everyone at BenBella Books—thank you, thank you, thank you! Adrienne Lang, thank you so much for shepherding this project along, working with the sales force, creating a beautiful cover, and making sure we were always in great hands. Jennifer Canzoneri and Lindsay Marshall, your marketing expertise has been invaluable. Thank you for making sure this book is presented in such a positive light and for working so hard on our behalf. Debbie Harmsen and Vy Tran, your editorial guidance and belief in this book have been incredible. Thank you for your passion, organization, and attention to detail. Monica Lowry, thank you for being so easy to work with and such an incredible production manager. We have been thrilled to work with such a professional! Jenna Sampson, thank you for being so conscientious and organized and for sharing our passion for the photos in this book. Alicia Kania, thank you for keeping us all organized and on the same page. And to Aida Herrera, thank you for taking such great care of us.

To Dr. Michael Ozner, thank you for your kindness, your belief in this book, and your belief and research in the health benefits of eating the Mediterranean way. Thank you for providing scientific proof of what I have always believed to be true. I am honored that you have lent us your voice and your support and that you have written the foreword for this book.

To our neighbors in Fanari, Greece, Pantelis, Aristoula, Stratos, and Vasia Tsimpiridis who shared their secret family recipes with us and kept us all fed very well. Not to mention putting up with endless shoots on the veranda during "Greek Siesta Time."

Sophia Chatzievgenidou, Jenny Katiou and Dimitra Katiou Maria and Vasso Koutrouba, Markella Moraitou, Maria and Kalliopi (Popi)

Halkia, for lending their helping hands and dishes.

The entire beach village of Fanari, Greece. Your warmth and *philotimia* at every turn made this experience wonderful. Thank you to all of you for coming together and helping us with anything and everything we needed to make this book a success. You are all the kindest, most welcoming people. Thank you for allowing the *"crazy workaholic Americans"* to infiltrate your sleepy little town over the summer and for welcoming us with open arms and laughter.

To Kosmas Doukakis, for sharing his secret "first boil the octopus in Coca-Cola" method for the very best grilled octopus and for treating us to his many delicacies at his idyllic seaside tavern.

The TV crew at Boo Productions: Alex Takis, Angelo Venetis, Spyros Vlachakis, Nikos Zogias, Kostas Koutelidakis, Kristina Anastopoulou, and my funny Greek American makeup artist BFF living in Athens, Peggy Karabilas.

To Barbara Walters and Bill Geddie. Thank you so much for your belief and for taking a chance on a young NYU graduate who was just starting out. Your early support of this book means the world to me.

To my family at *Home & Family* on the Hallmark Channel. Thank you for being so supportive of my passion for my Greek heritage and for celebrating this book with me.

To Rita Thompson at HARPO, thank you for your support on this project.

Everyone at the fabulous and chic Athens Hilton Galaxy Bar for allowing us to shoot our piece there for OWN and for taking such good care of all of us—keeping us well-fed and hydrated! Vasillis Karayianopoulos, Tsambika Tsakiri, Gregoris Mitrakis, Dimitris Zarmakoupis. The lovely people at the most amazing restaurant in Athens, *Elias Gi,* for opening their doors to us and feeding us one of the best meals I have ever eaten in my life. Jimmy Kolovakis, Mary Kolovaki, and Victoria Prifti, that is an evening I will never forget.

To my friends and neighbors who have been my taste testers along the way. Jeffrey Wilson, Allison Stoltz, Brandi Huzzie, Norma Ball, Ashley Ragland, Angie Linares, Joseph Place, Maximino Altamirano, thank you.

Very special thanks to Ford Lowcock, Josh Withers, Craig Mohr, Steve Moulton, Melanie Shatto, Oscar at ICON Photo, Linda Rakolta, and Joel Raven. Ralph Fowler, thank you for your beautiful design. This book would not have been possible without all of the love and support of the people mentioned here. And to you who have taken the time to sit down with this book and plan a meal in the spirit of Greece, we thank you from the bottom of our hearts and wish you and yours good health and a great appetite as you enjoy these recipes!

About the Authors

DEBBIE MATENOPOULOS is a two-time Emmy nominee for her celebrated work as a TV host and journalist. She began her career in entertainment at the age of seventeen when she was hired by MTV. At twenty-one, she became youngest person in history to hold a permanent position on daytime network television when Barbara Walters handpicked her to be one of the first five cohosts of ABC's venerable talk show *The View*. After *The View*, Debbie went on to host shows for FOX (*Good Day Live*), the Style Network (the Emmy-nominated *Instant Beauty Pageant*), and E! (*Live from the Red Carpet*; *The Daily 10*; *Fashion Police*), among others. She was instrumental in the launch of the TV Guide channel as one of its first on-camera hosts, and she has appeared in several films. For two years, Debbie served as cohost and special correspondent for CBS Television's *The Insider*. She is currently a regular contributor to Hallmark's *Home & Family*. Most important to Debbie is her Greek heritage. She is the first member of her all-Greek family to have been born in the United States. A Greek American girl at heart, her love of family, love of tradition, and love of her Greek culture is essential to her above all else. She is passionate about sharing her experience with food, health, wellness, and family.

PETER CAPOZZI is a writer, producer, and director. His television career began at the age of nineteen when he was hired by Martha Stewart Living Television. His work has been featured on HBO, Encore, Lifetime, and the Style Network. He has written, produced, and directed for the Independent Film Channel, E! News, and CBS Television (*Entertainment Tonight*; *The Insider*), among others. He has also worked extensively in digital and new media. Peter is the executive producer of the hit Public Television/PBS series *Jazzy Vegetarian*, the only plant-based cooking show currently being produced for broadcast television. He is also an avid yogi and a certified teacher of Kundalini yoga.

Index

S